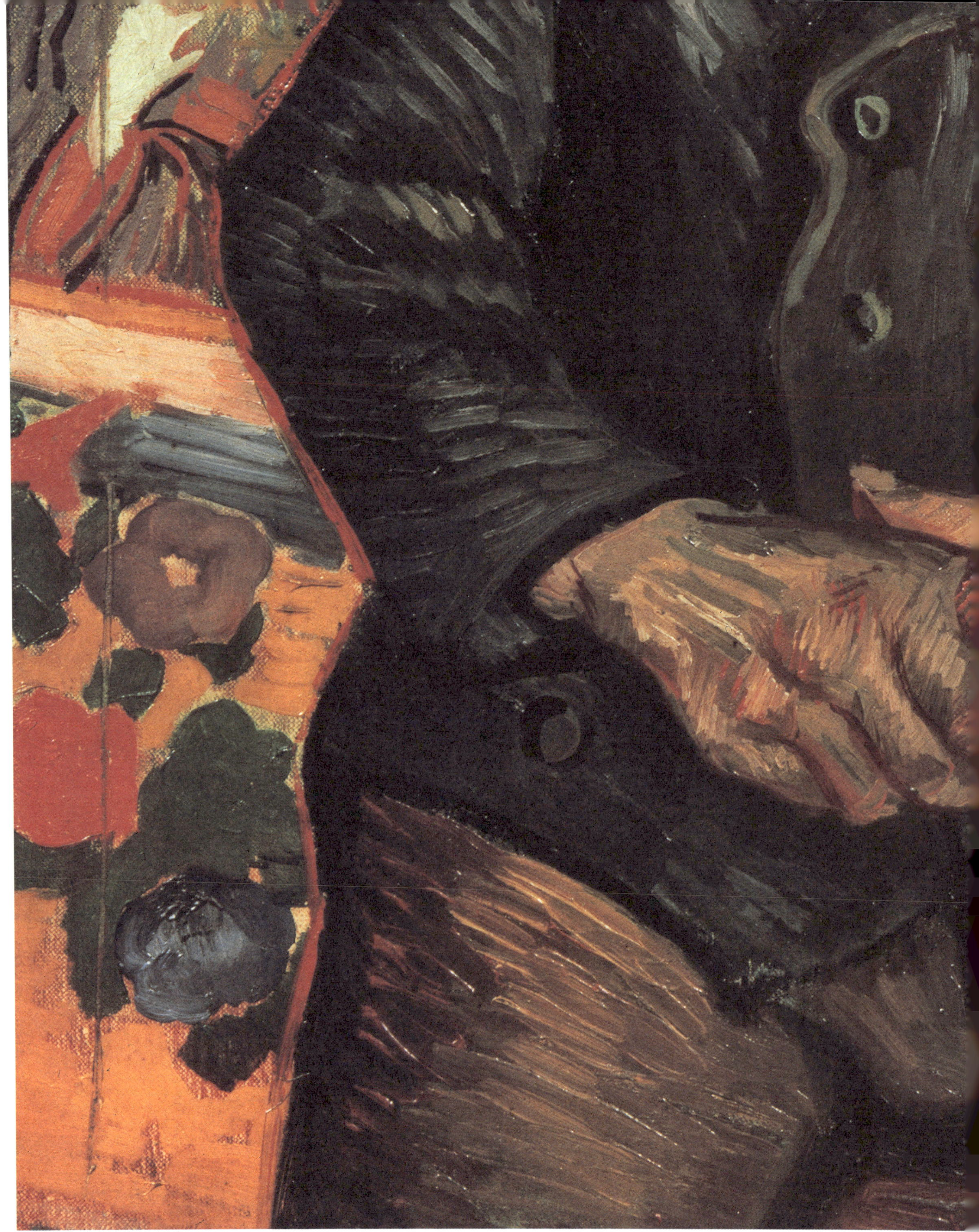

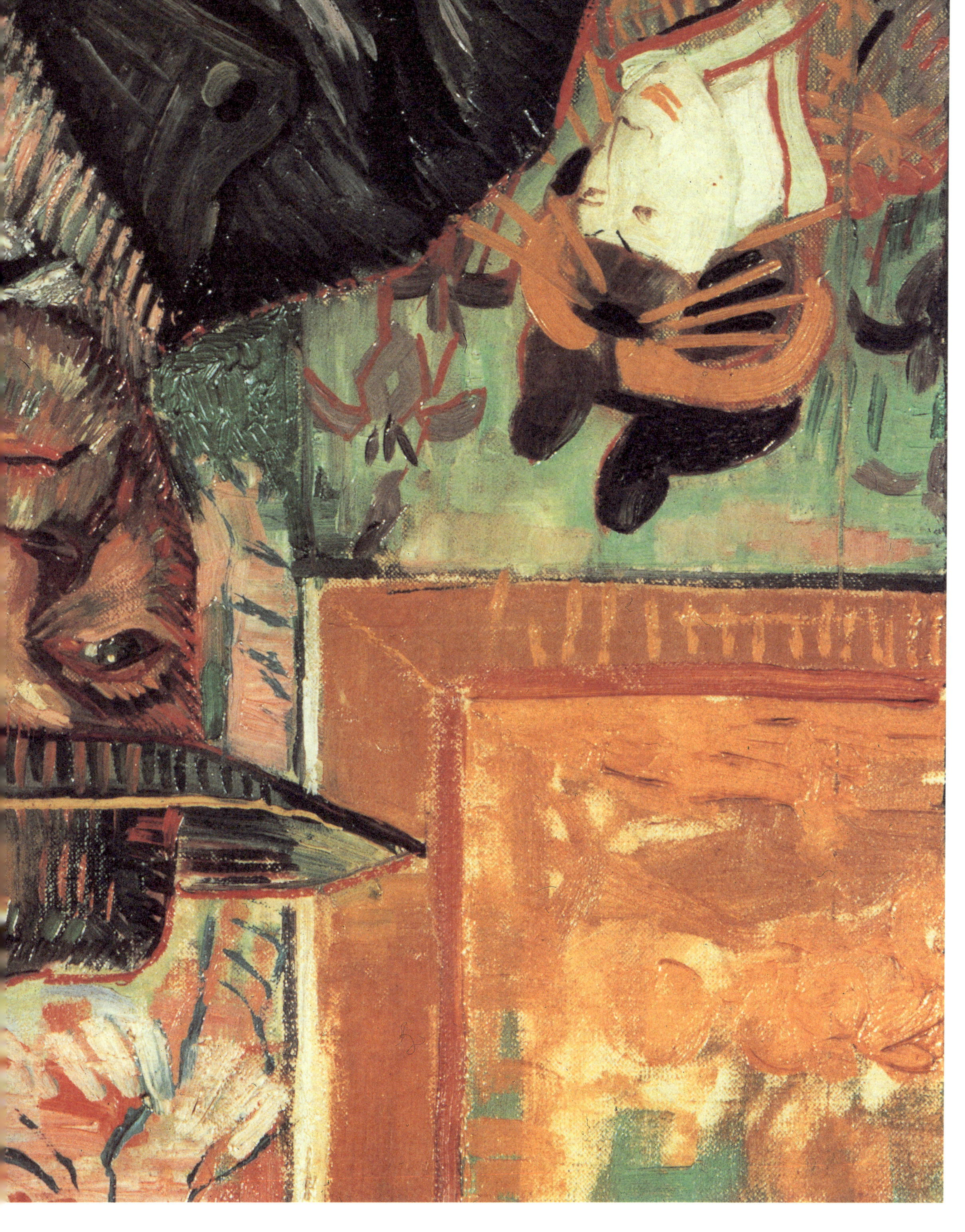

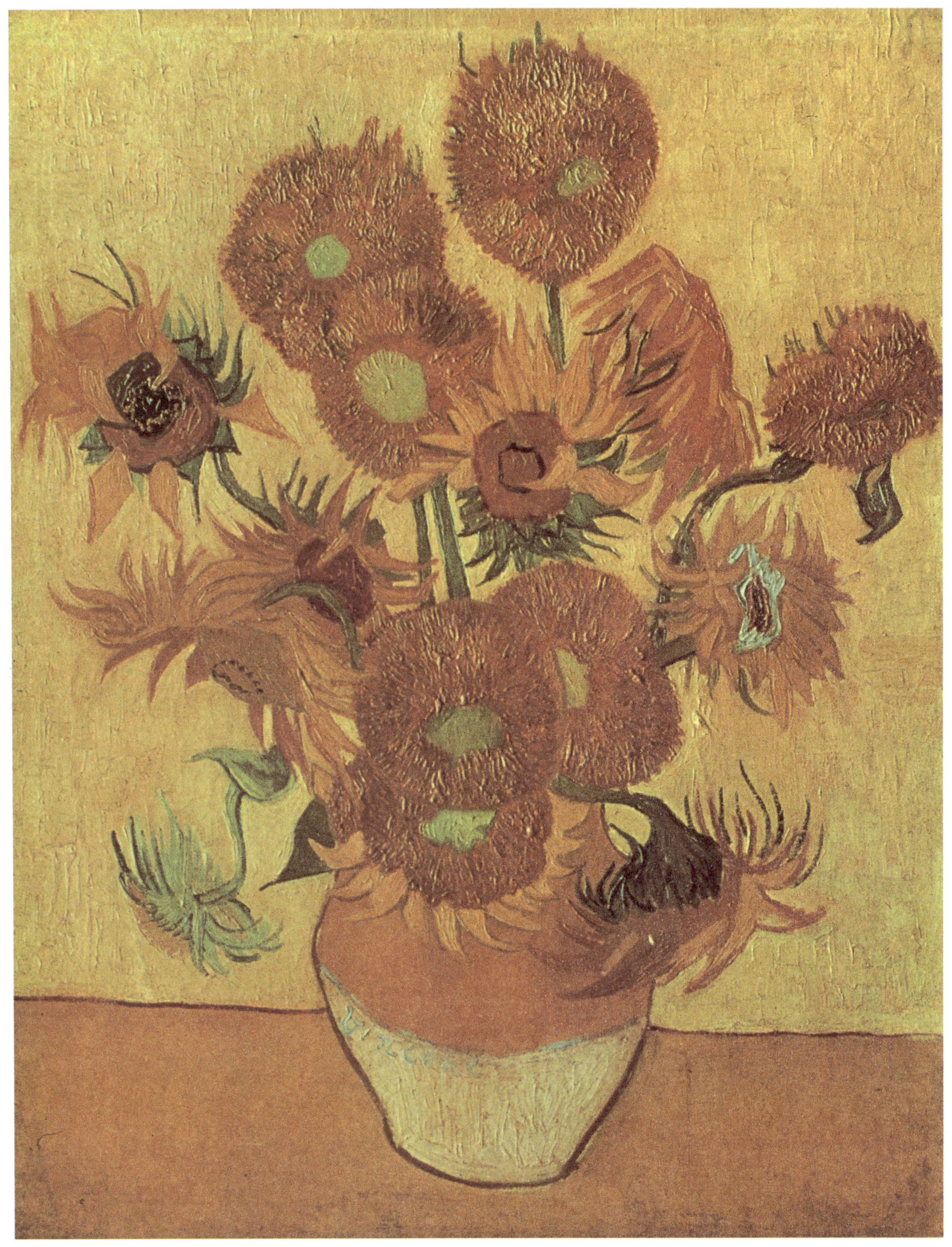
Vincent

VINCENT VAN GOGH

a RizzoliQuadrifolio

RIZZOLI
NEW YORK

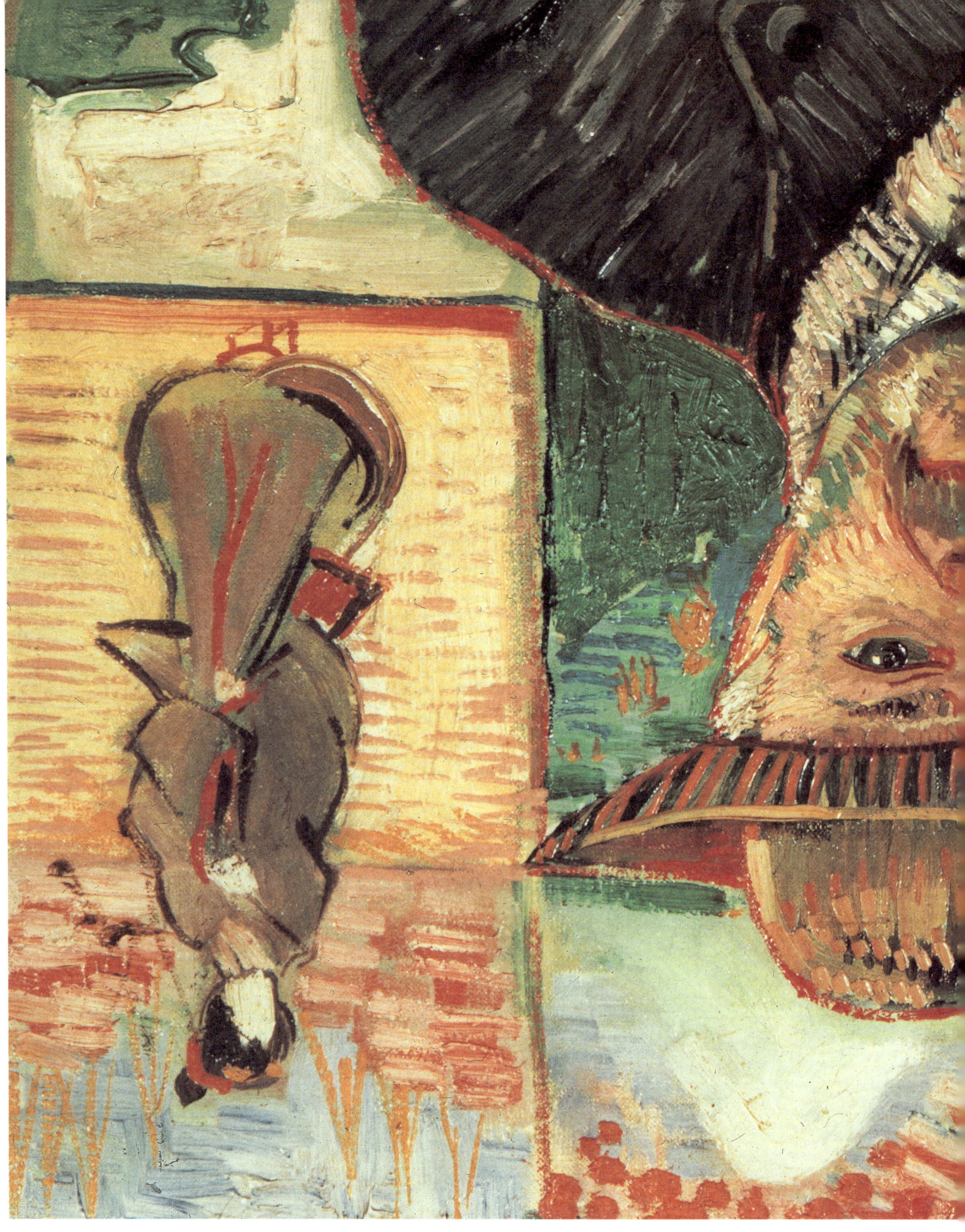

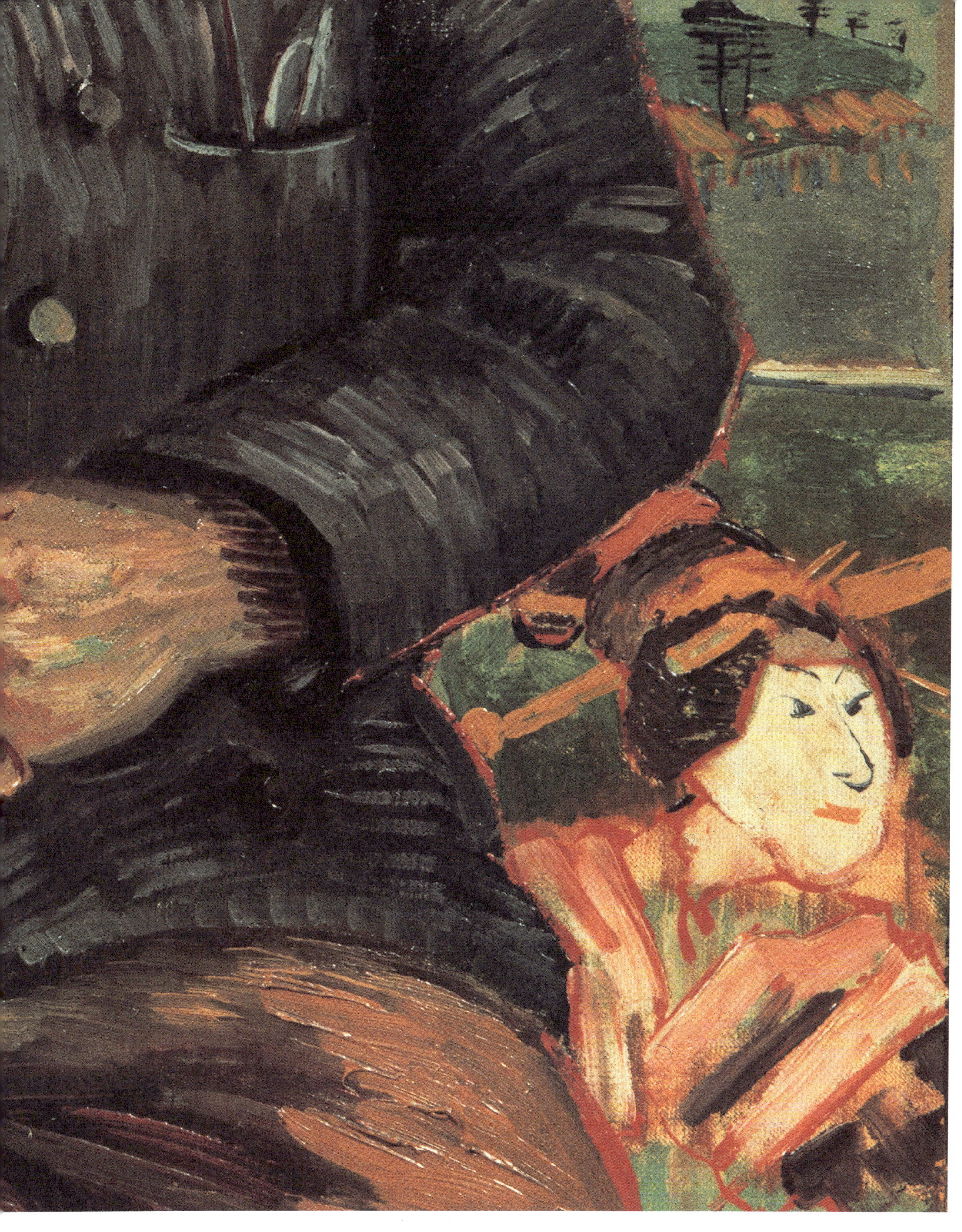

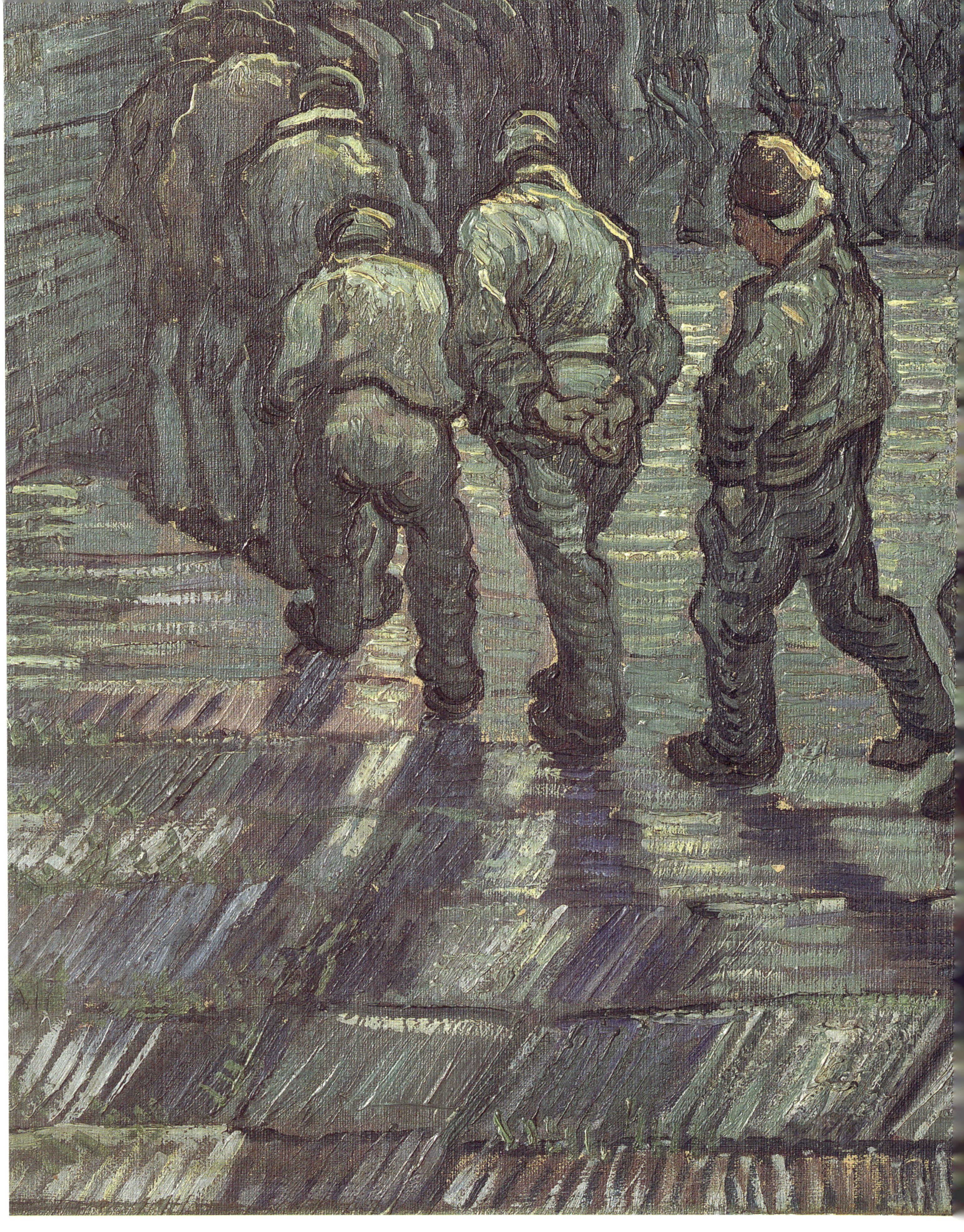

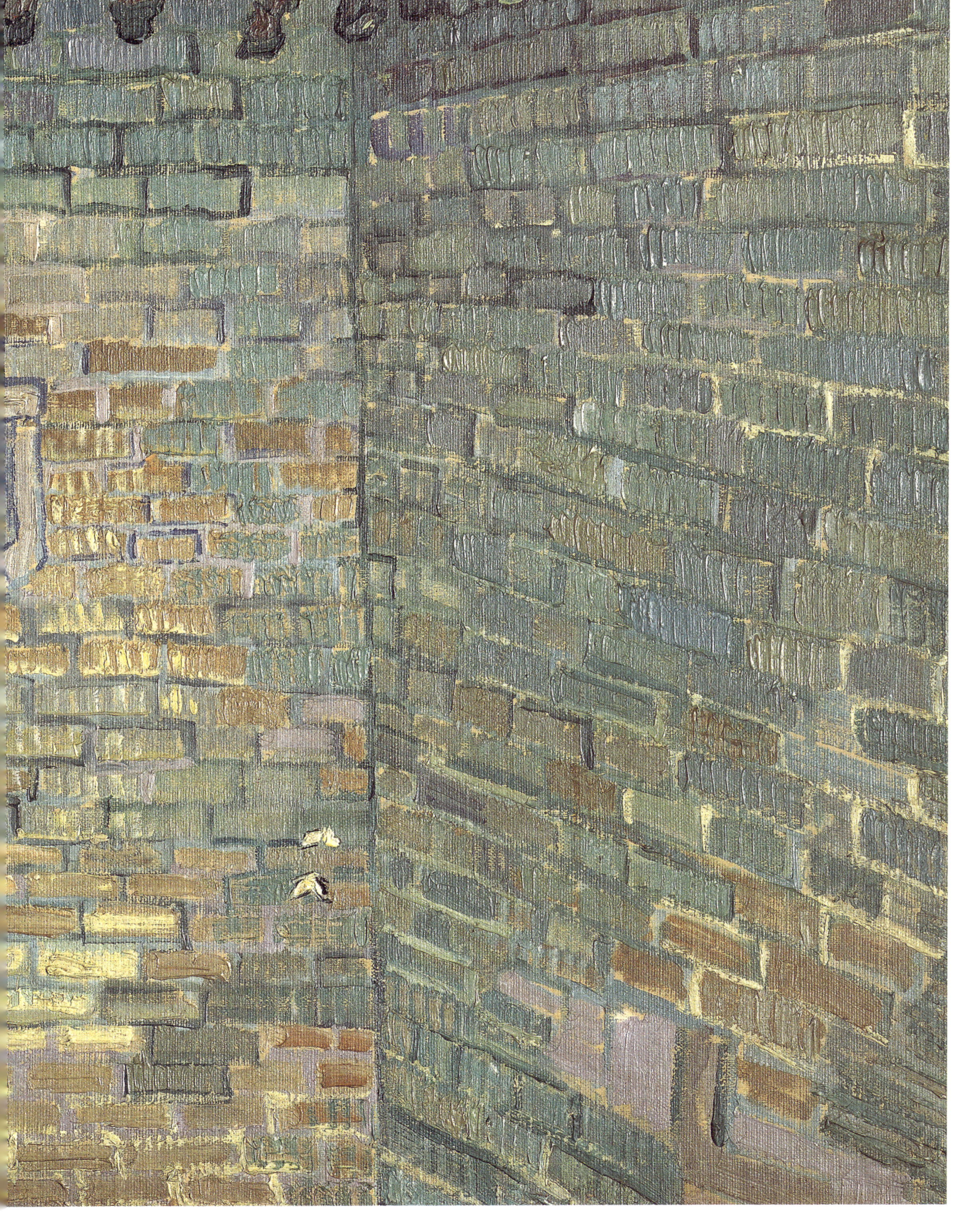

In order to paint, van Gogh had to have the world right in front of him: perhaps no other painter's eye has been so consumed by the need to interrogate every form, every color, every vibration of the light. The son of a Protestant pastor, he began to study theology, but terminated his studies in 1869 to become an apprentice at the Parisian art dealers Goupil and Co., first in the Hague, then in London, and finally in Paris, until he was fired in 1876 because of his difficulty in dealing with clients.

As his inability to accept social rules grew worse, he left for Belgium in 1878 and devoted himself to missionary work. However, he was forced to stop the following year on the orders of the religious authorities. Yet it was here, among the miners of the Borinage, that his vocation for painting emerged: in the faces wracked with pain and fatigue of those men who spent their lives in the harsh reality of the coal mines, he recognized the living image of Christ's suffering and everything he saw automatically became part of his artistic imagery.

In 1880 he went to Brussels and enrolled in the Academy there. But his desire to paint directly from nature was irresistible. In December 1883 he joined his family at Neunen, in the region of Brabant in the Netherlands, and, no longer tormented by a lack of money, devoted himself unstintingly to painting *en plein air*. Here he created his first masterpieces, such as *The Potato Eaters*, which represents the synthesis of a series of studies of heads of peasants and artisans absorbed in their humble work. In these pictures, with their marked social content, the influence of the realism of the second half of the nineteenth century is clear: in particular Daumier and his exaggeration of expression to the point of realistic deformation and Courbet's use of color in an expressive rather than naturalistic way.

Following the death of his father, his misanthropic attitude strirred the hostility of the village's inhabitants, and departure was inevitable: van Gogh, driven by a desire to expand the modest range of themes offered by the countryside, moved to Antwerp and then, in February 1886, to Paris, where he stayed with his brother Theo. The city, where the eighteenth-century *querelle des anciens et modernes* still raged, was inundated with a flood of "isms": impressionism, symbolism, cloisonnism, synthetism, divisionism, signs of the revolutionary impetus of the modern, but also symptoms of the marginal position of the new art.

In Paris van Gogh shook off the heavy burden of the years of his training and moved closer, in his handling of images and color, to the great art of the impressionists. In 1888 he went to live at Arles, in the south of France, where he was dazzled by the light of the Mediterranean. His style was enriched with a new brilliance of color, laid on the canvas in thick and distinct brushstrokes. In September of the same year the artist realized his dream of setting up a house of his own, the "yellow house"—the color was meant to identify him as an artist of the south—which he intended to be the home of the *Atelier du midi*, a community of artists who would renew the very foundations of art, pursuing the utopian project of creating a better world. If Gauguin had worked out the technical principles of what was to become expressionism at the Breton village of Pont-Aven, then it can also be said that van Gogh discovered its moral principles in Arles.

Gauguin joined him there in October 1888, but the friendship between the two painters lasted just a few dramatic months before breaking down over the incompatibility of their aesthetic ideas and above all their lifestyles. Forced to acknowledge the failure of a utopia to which he had devoted so much of his energies, van Gogh fell prey to recurrent bouts of depression and fits of violence directed against himself, culminating in his cutting off the lobe of one ear.

In May 1889, he left the "yellow house" which had been damaged by a flood and decided to have himself admitted to the lunatic asylum of Saint-Paul-de-Mausole, a converted Augustinian monastery in the vicinity of Saint-Rémy. The artist, convinced of his inability to adapt to the rules of society, consciously took refuge in madness. His work grew feverish and passionate: he poured all the drama of his complex existential crisis into every subject he painted, and not just his numerous self-portraits. In May 1890 he left Saint-Rémy for Auvers-sur-Oise where, after a brief period during which he seemed to be on the mend, he began to suffer from increasingly frequent fits of madness that inspired a visionary style of painting, filled with unprecedented violence. In July of the same year, in a field of ripe wheat flooded with sunlight, the artist shot himself in the breast with a pistol.

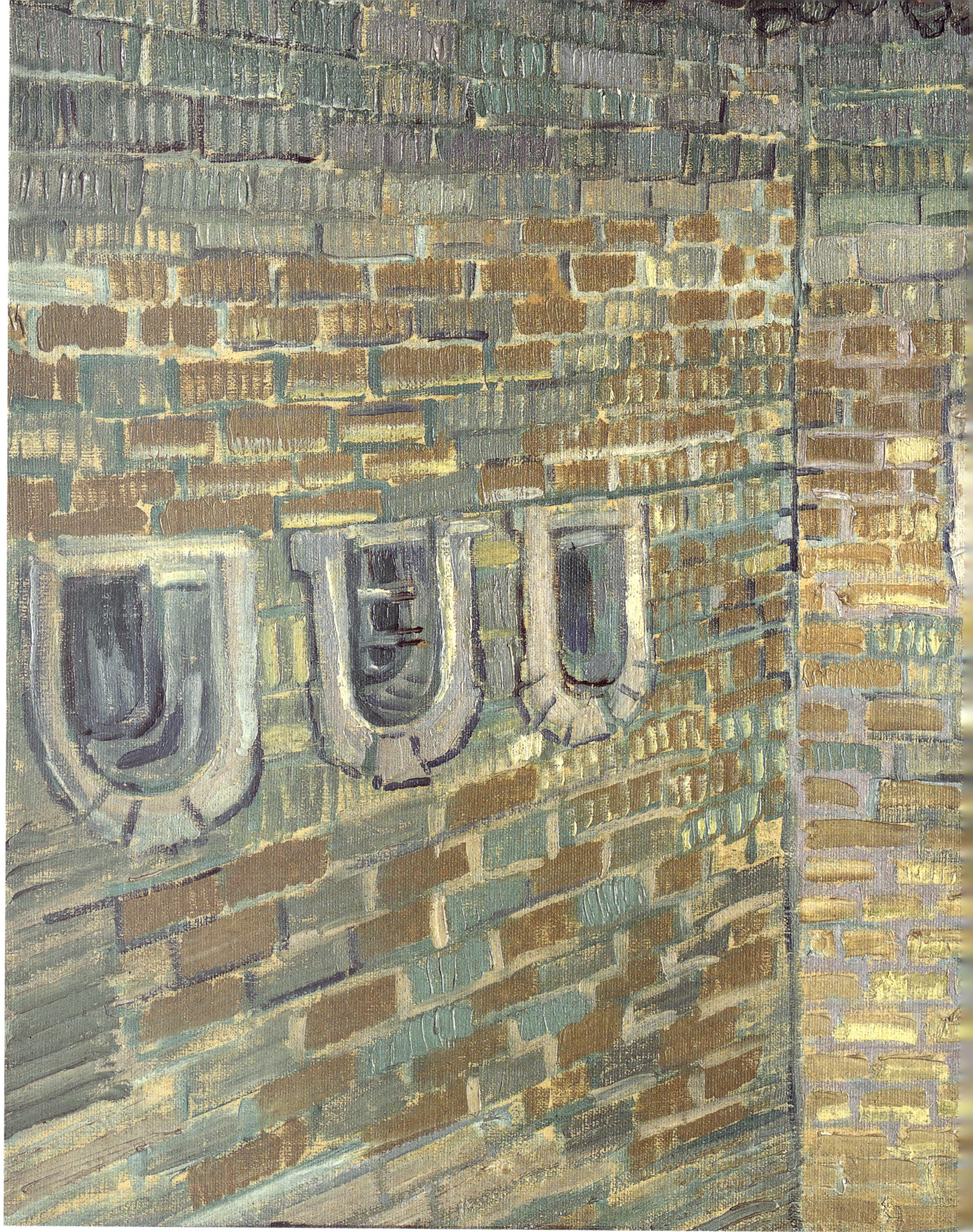

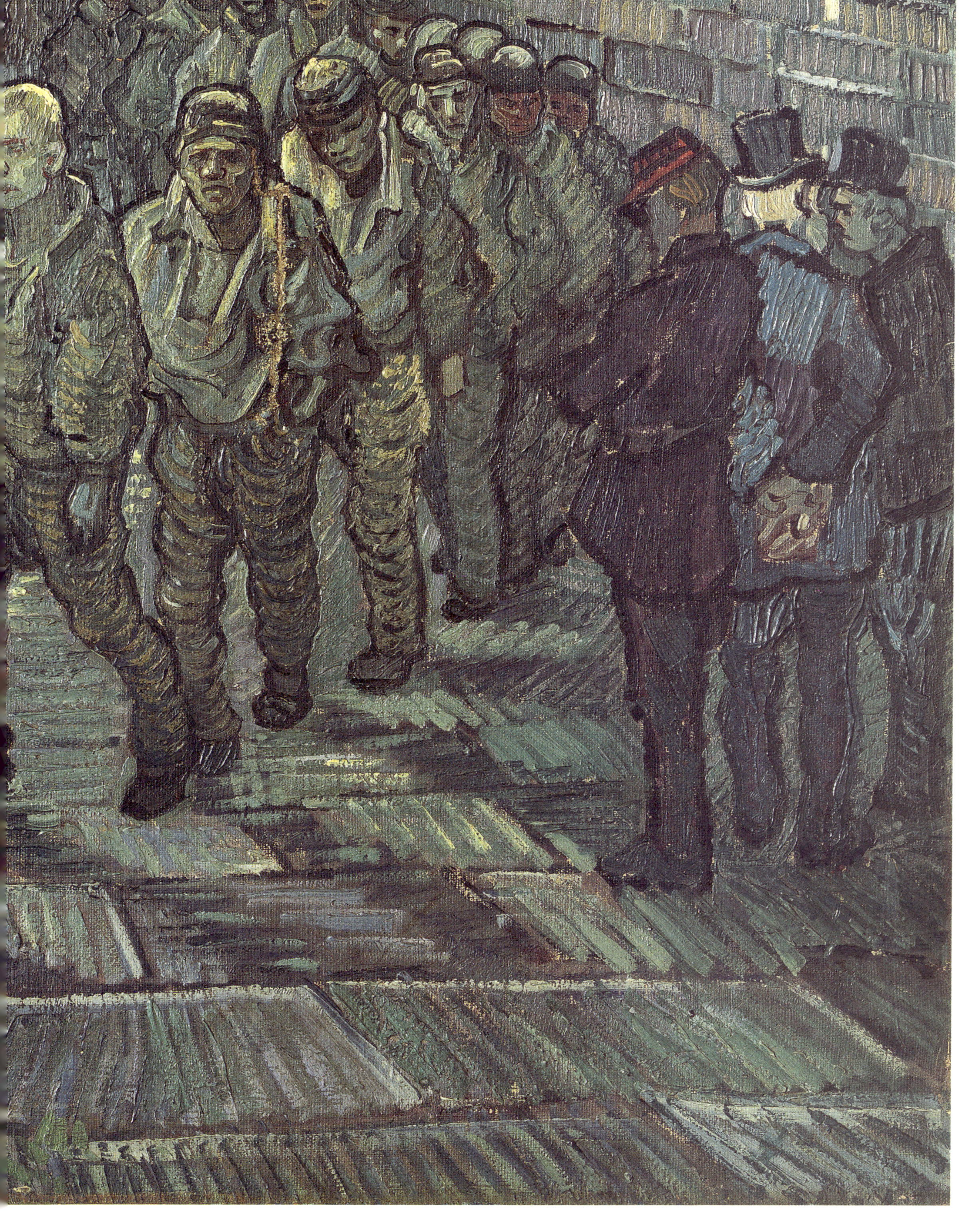

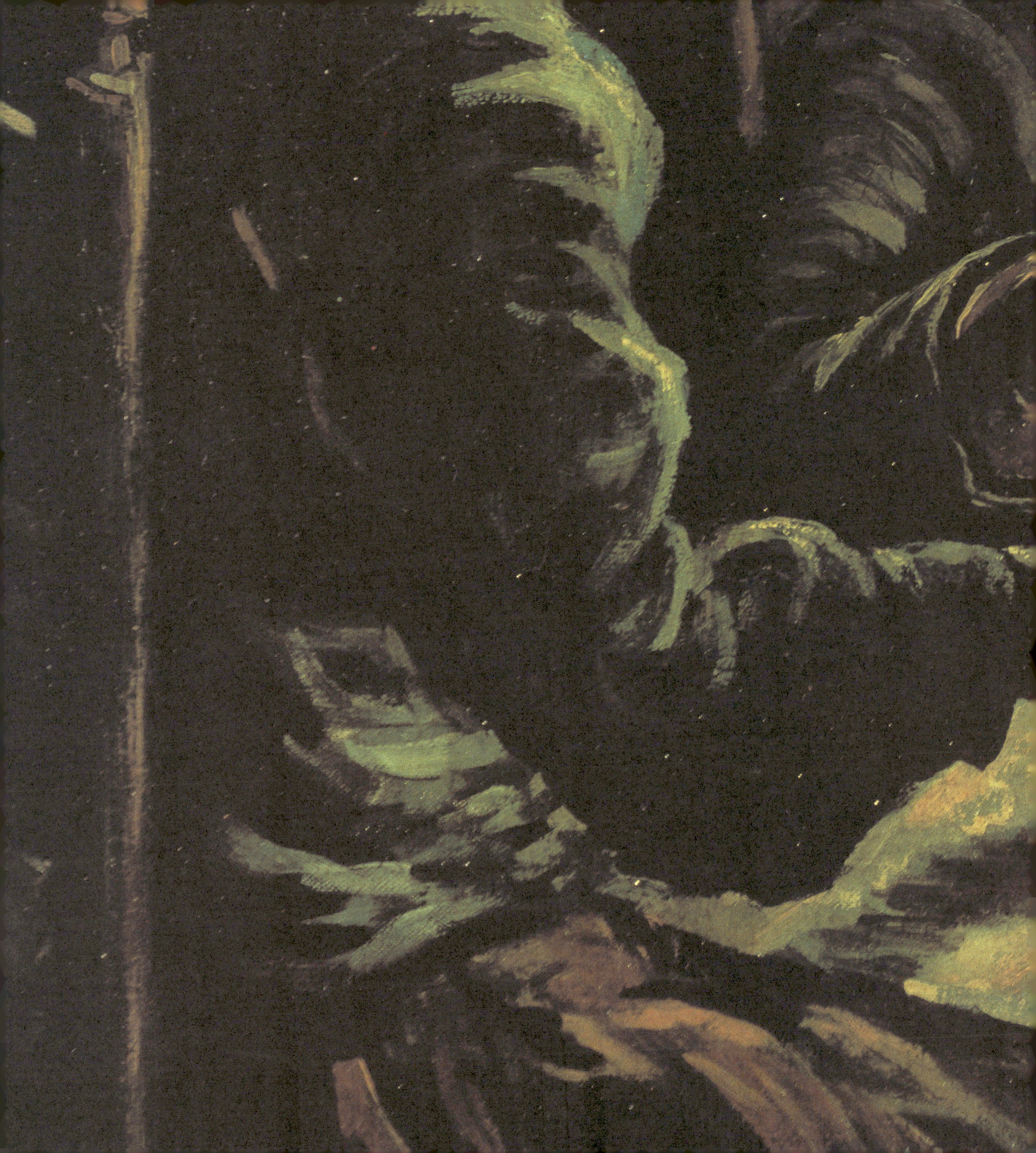

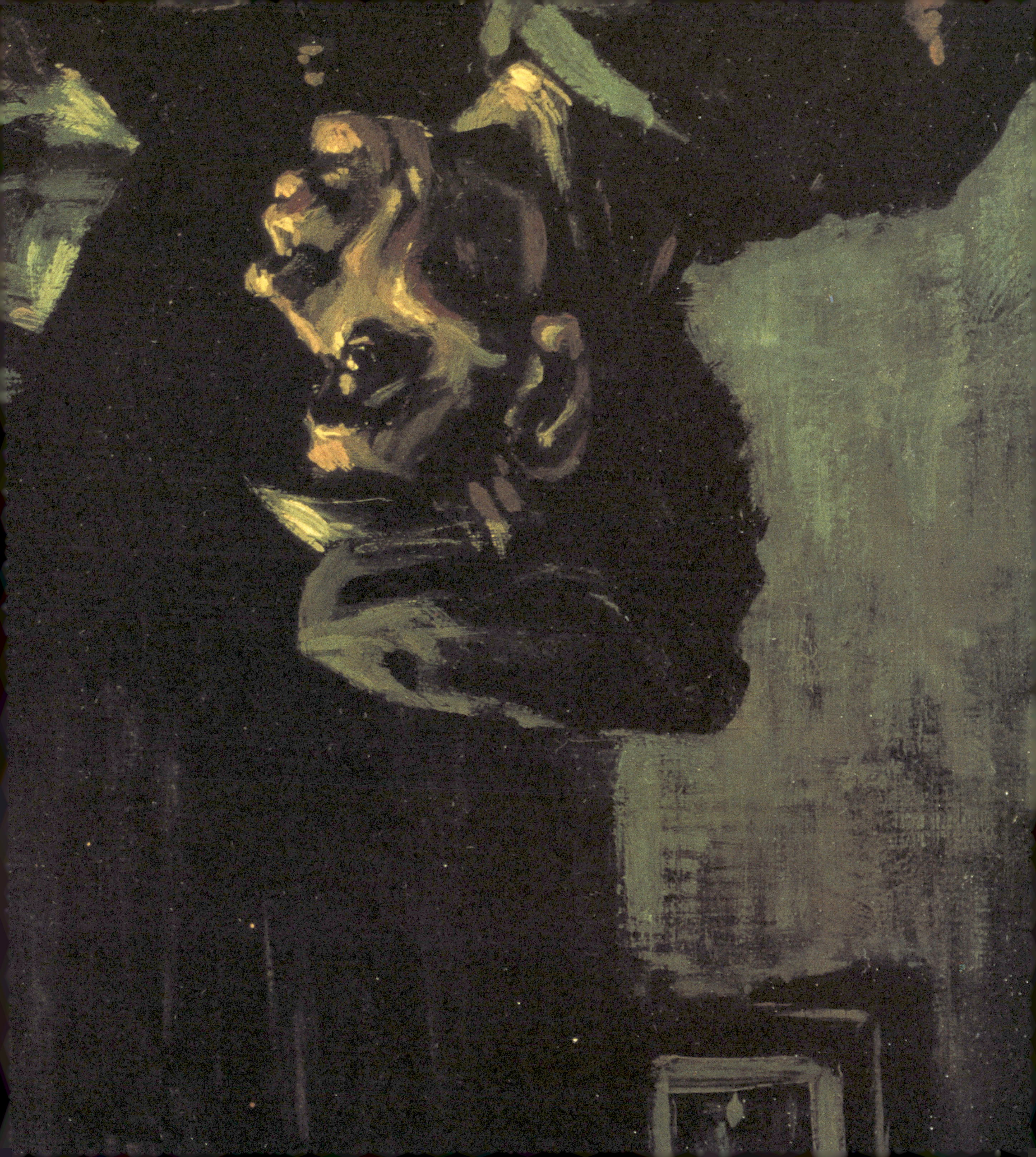

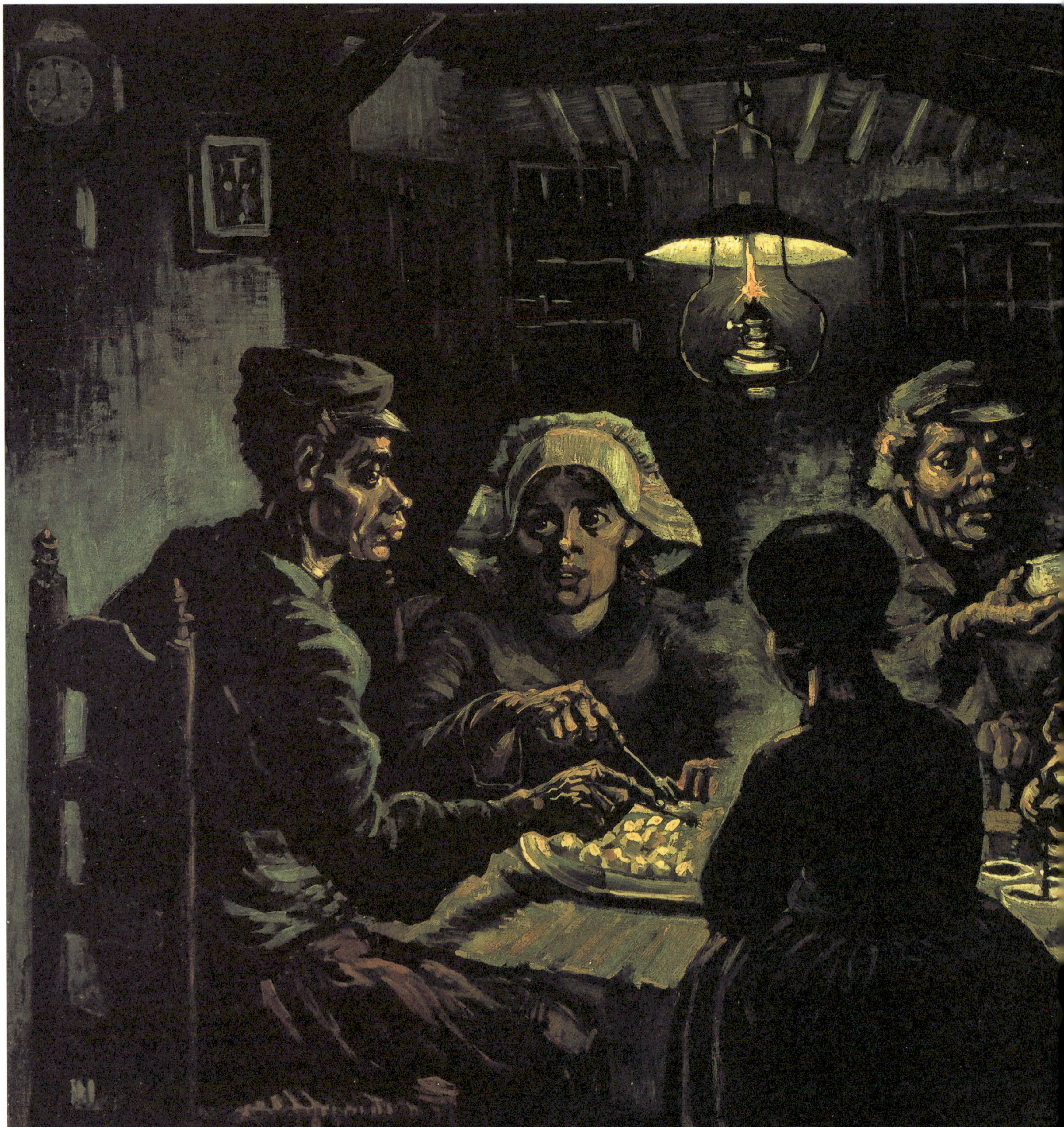

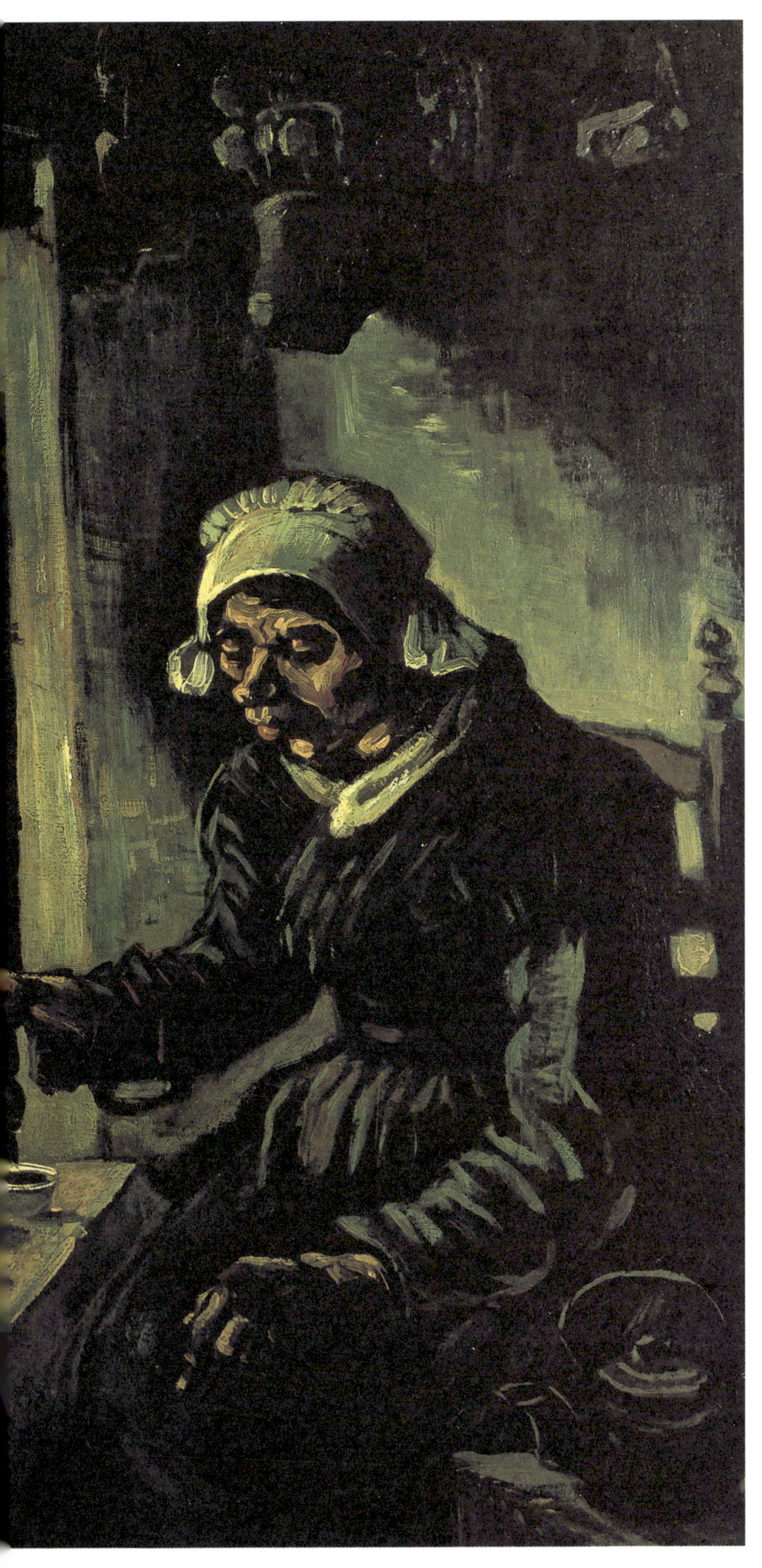

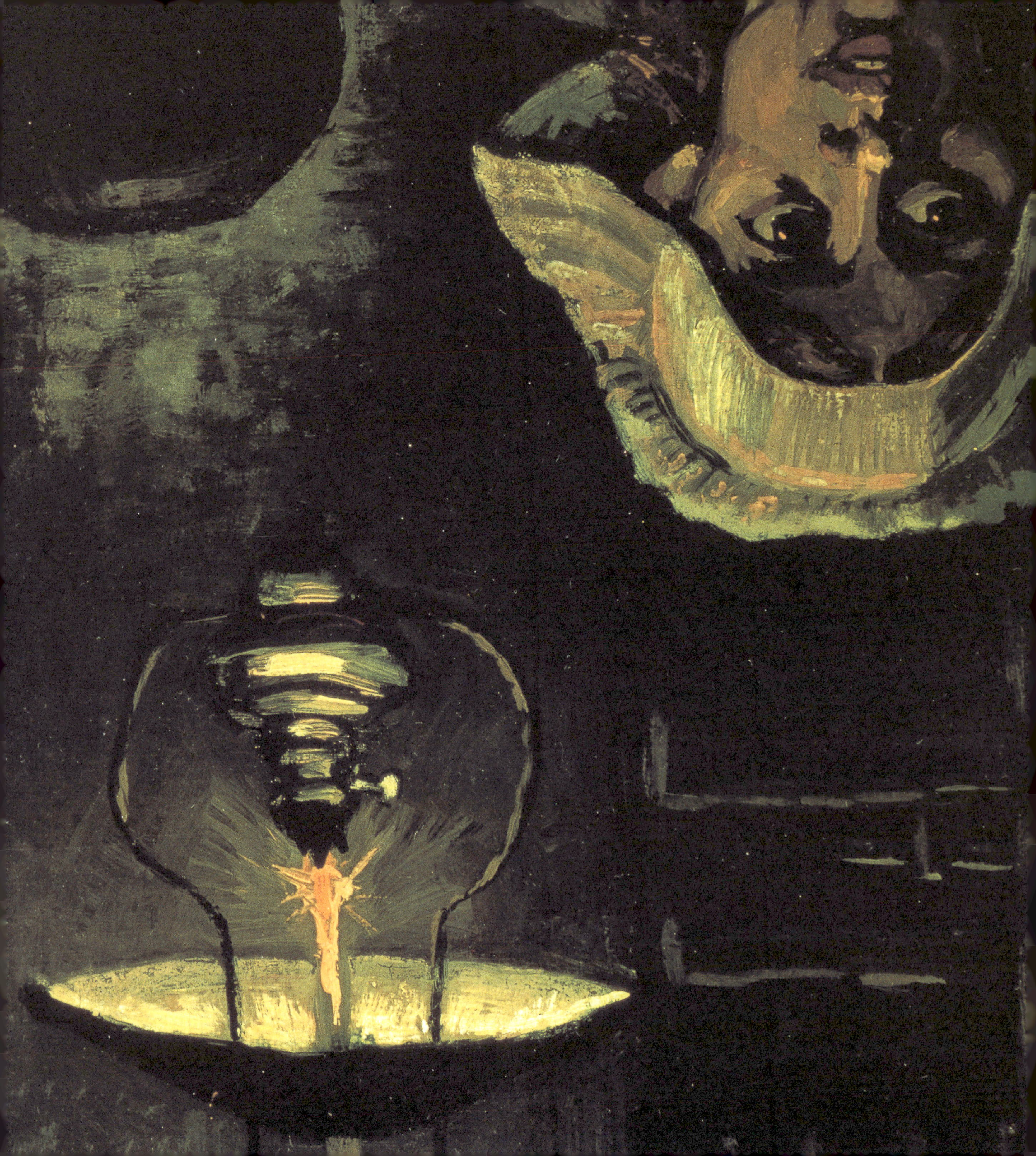

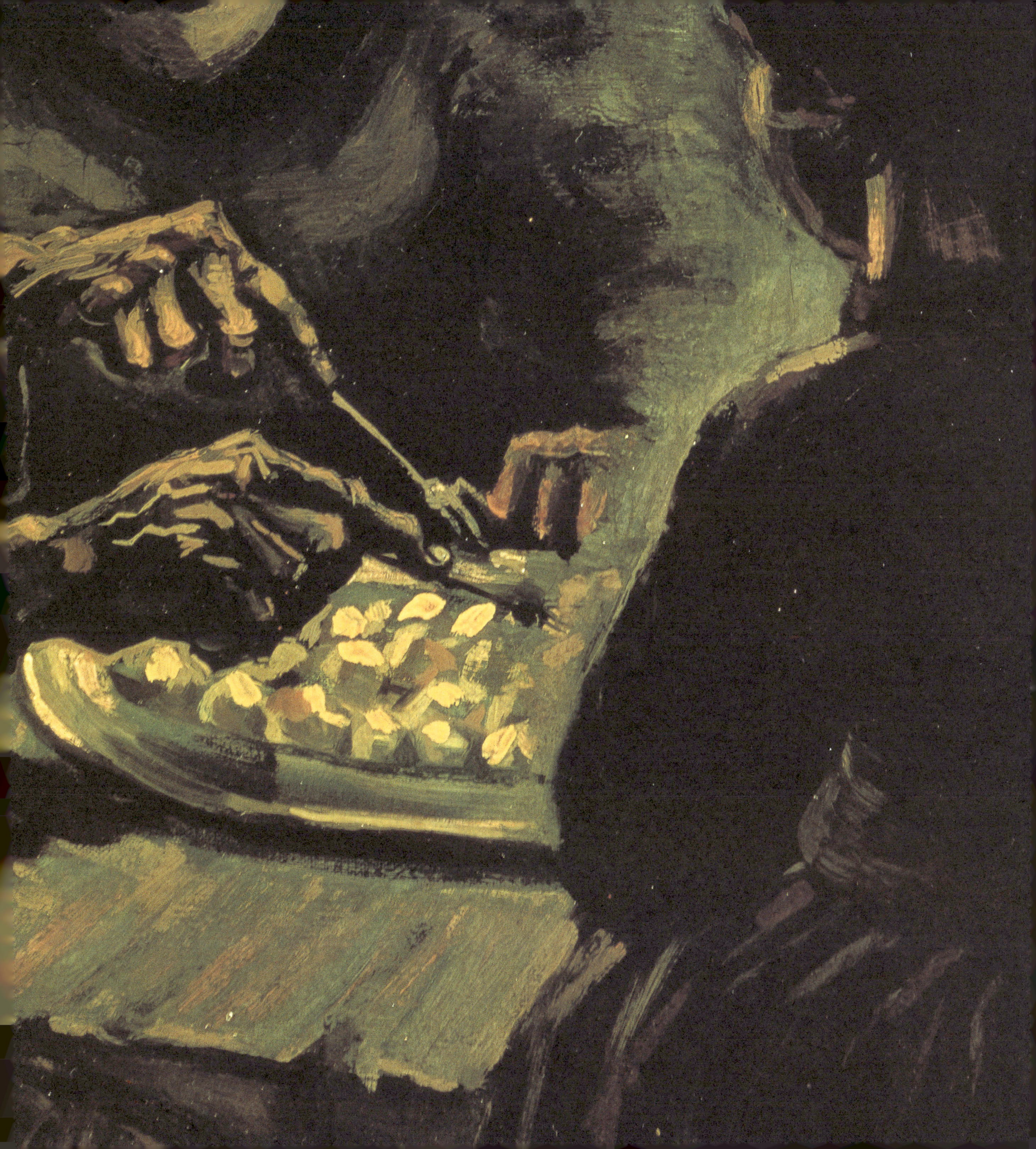

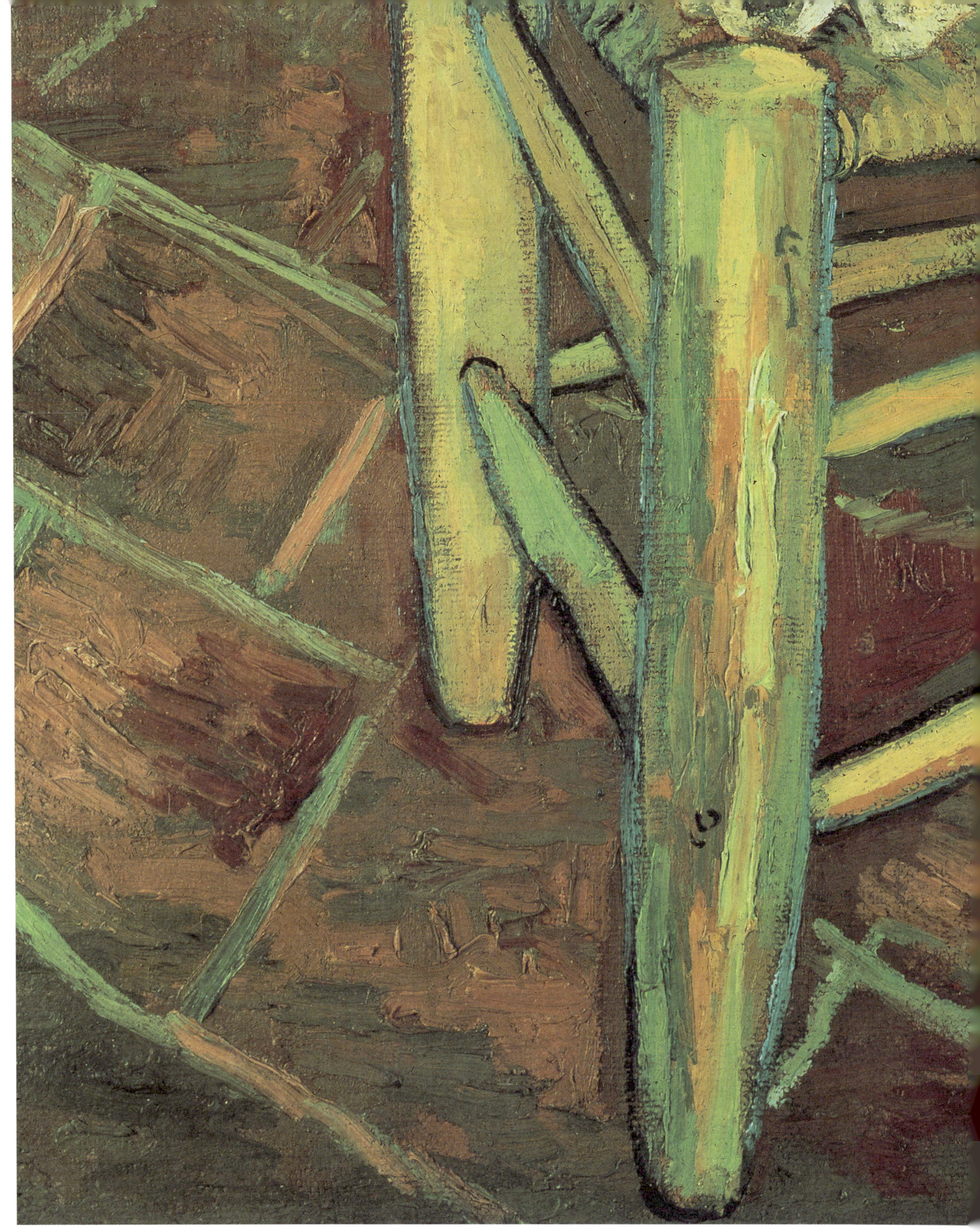

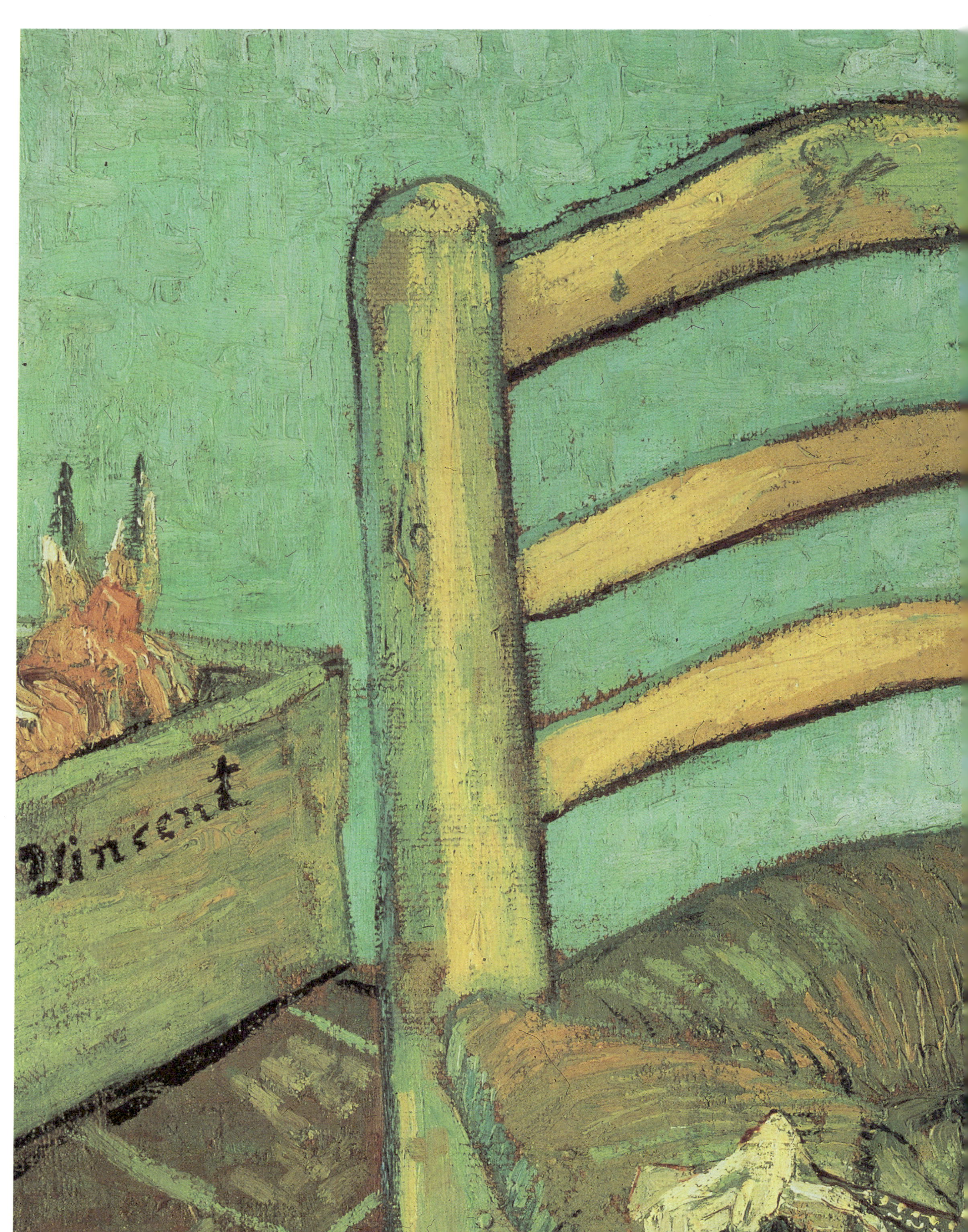
Vincent

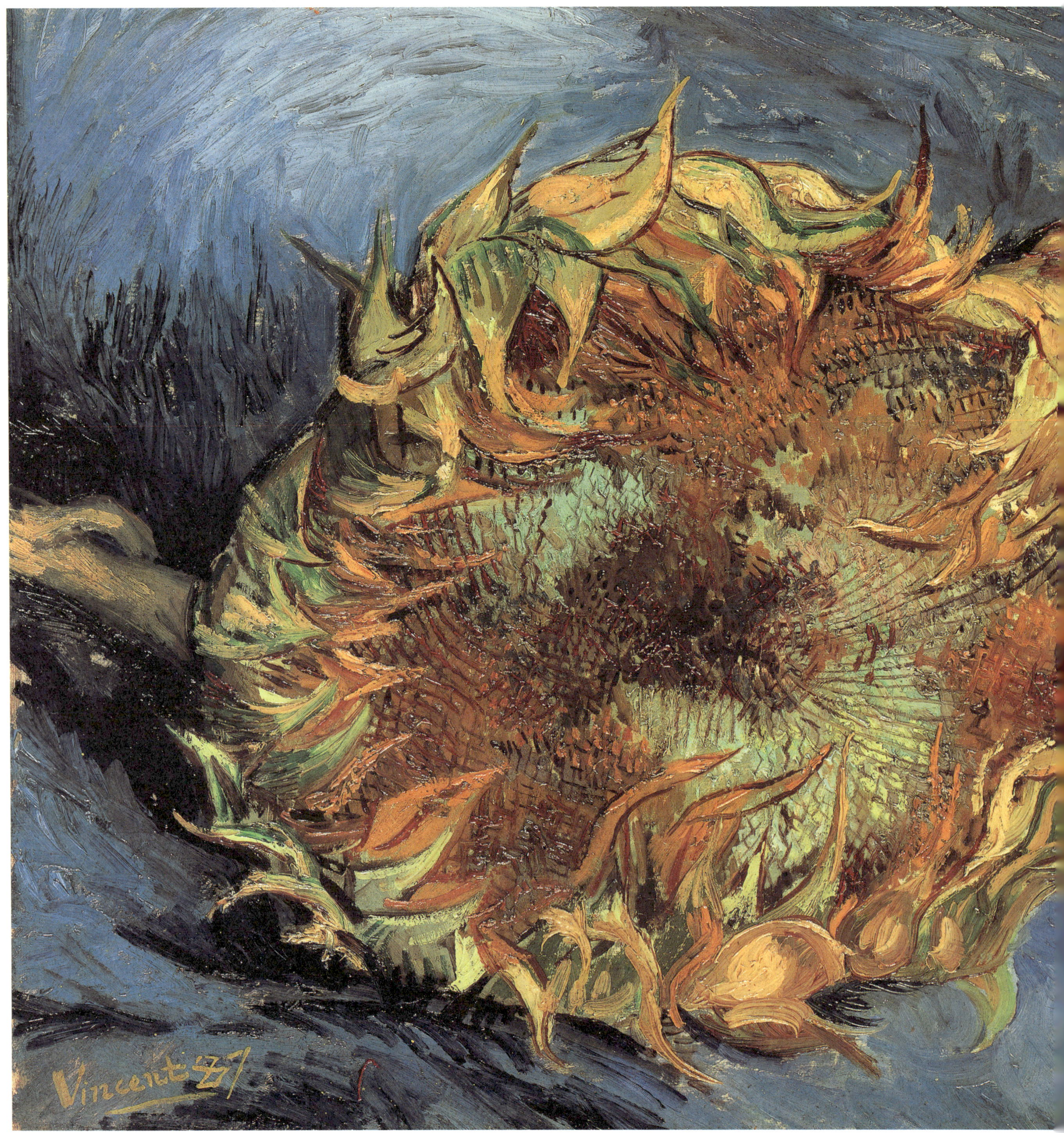
Vincent 87

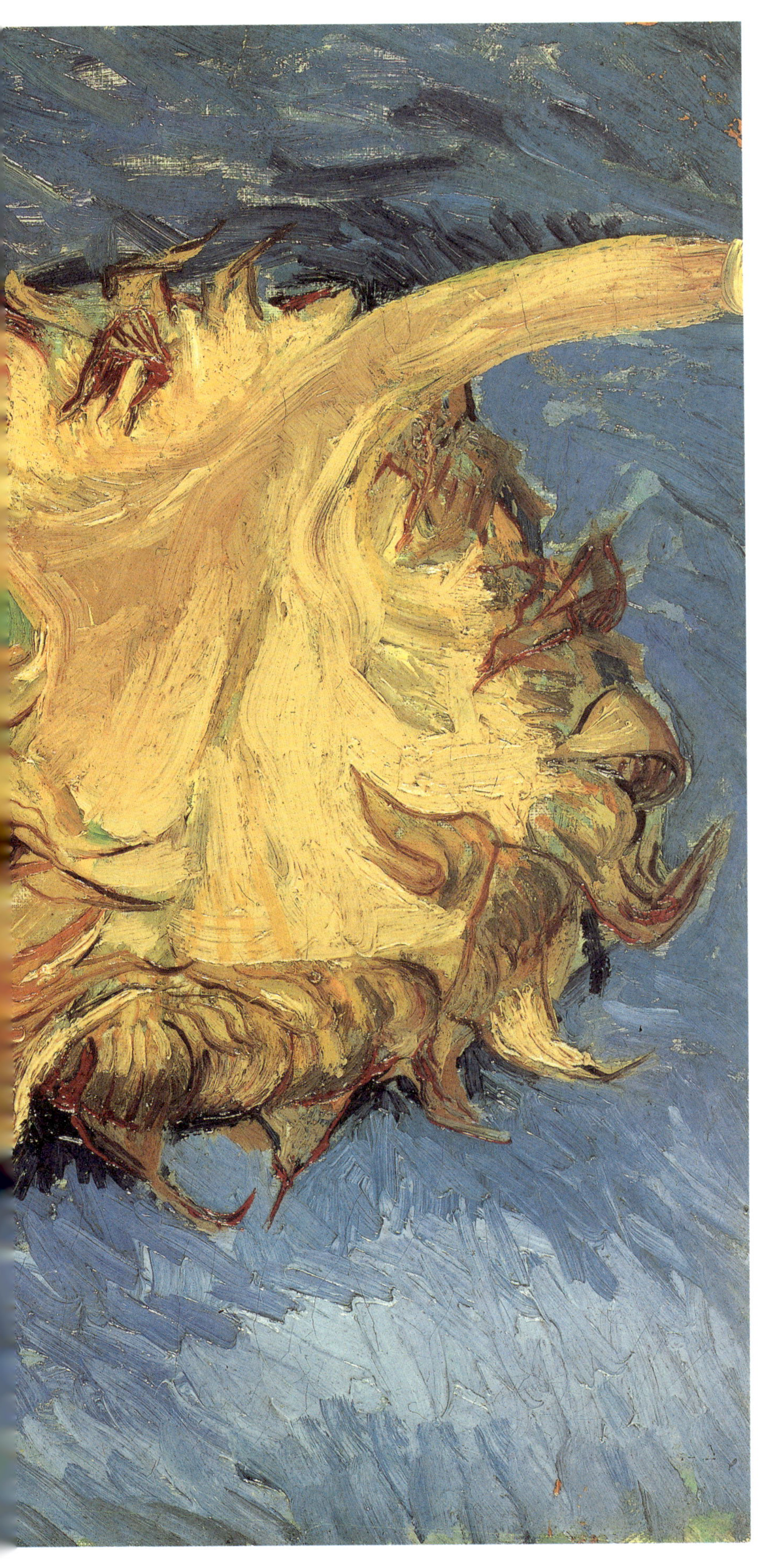

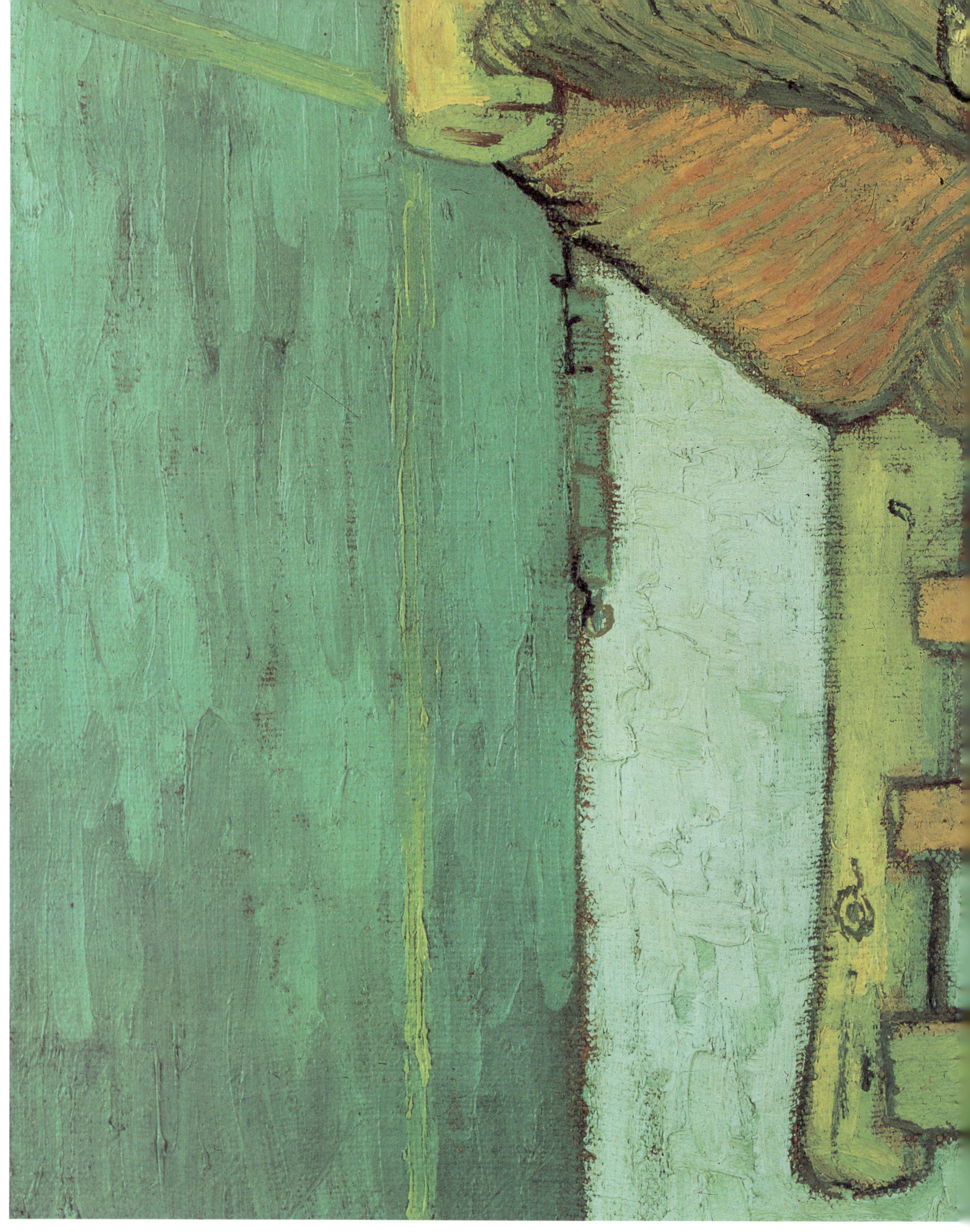

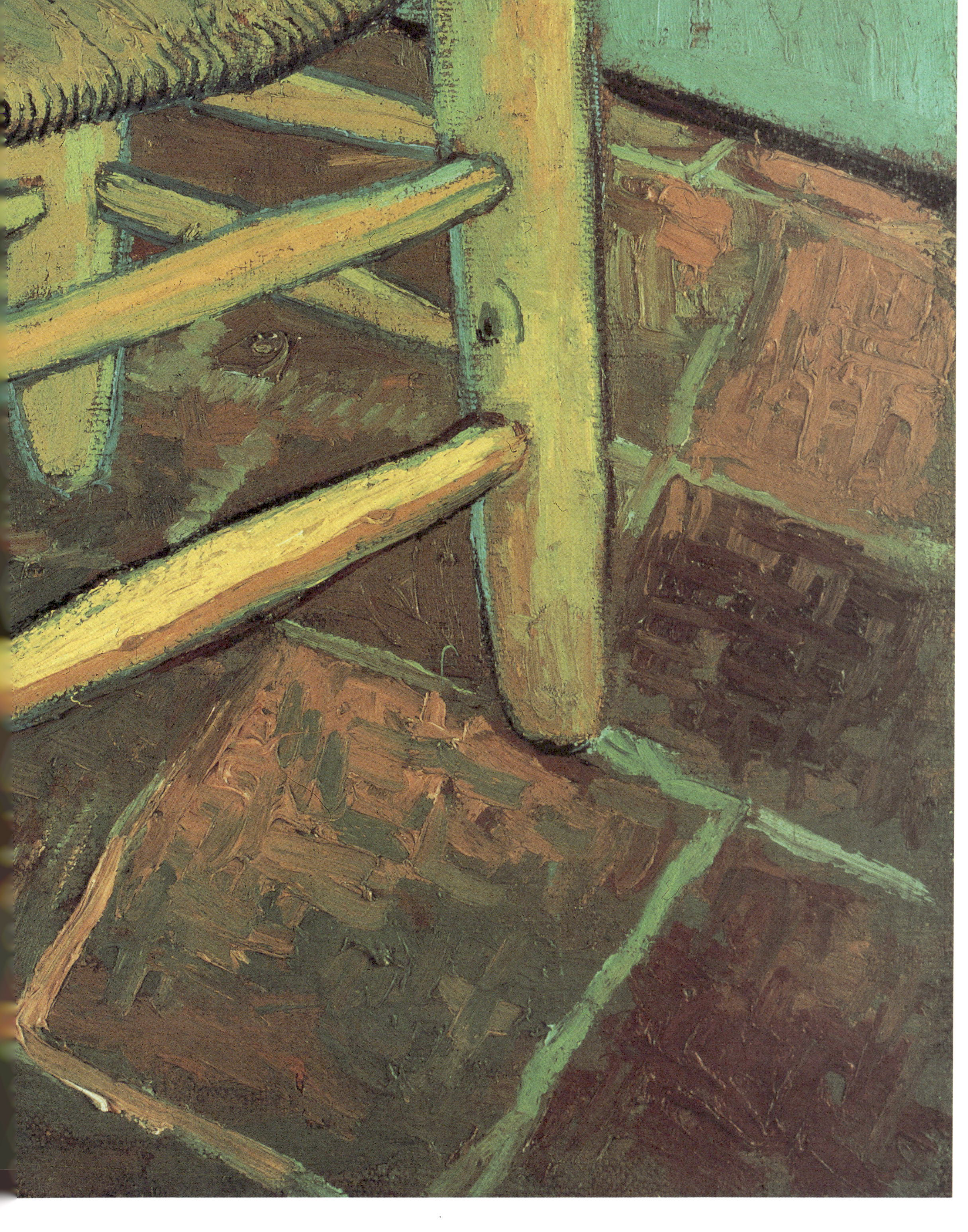

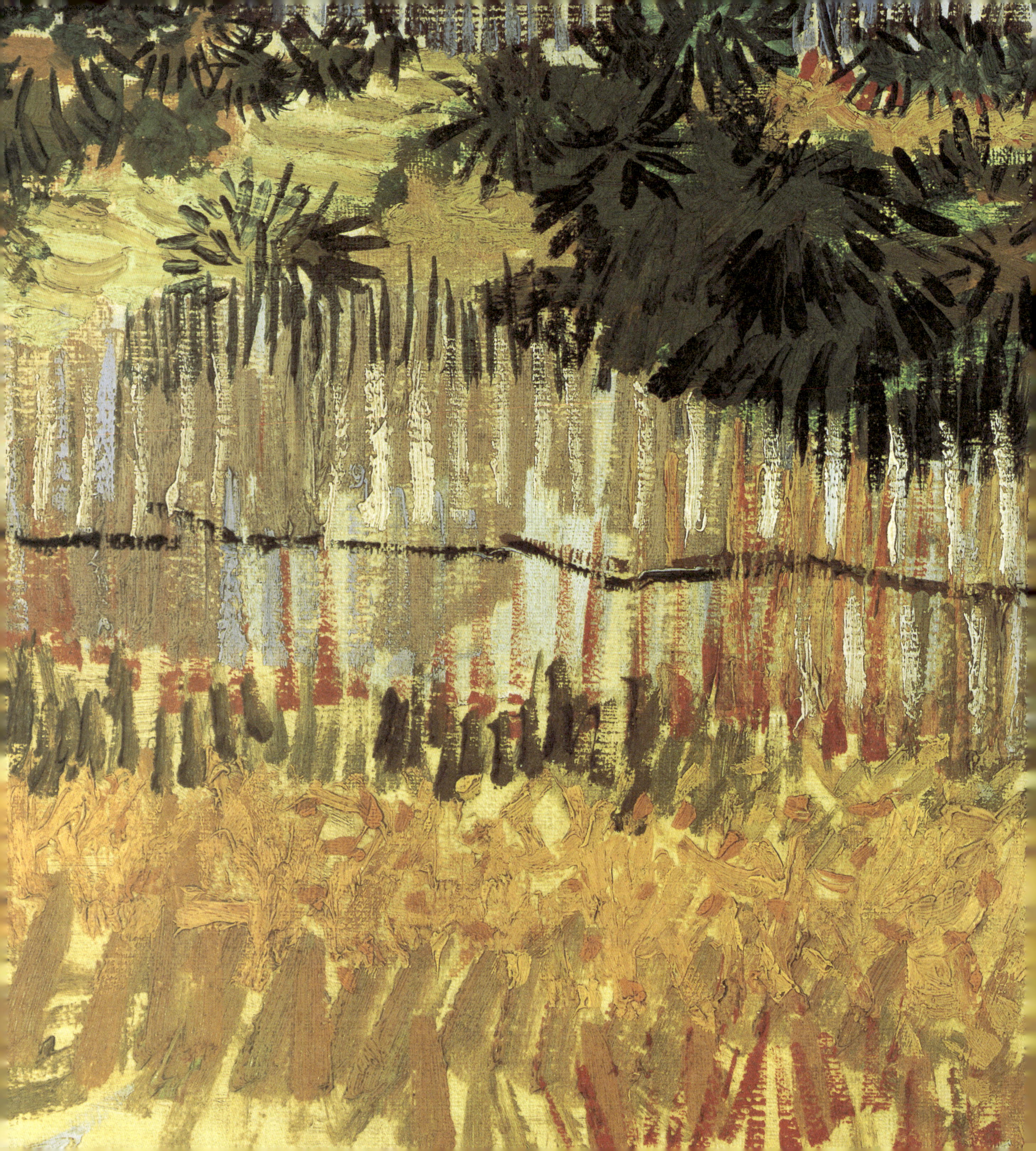

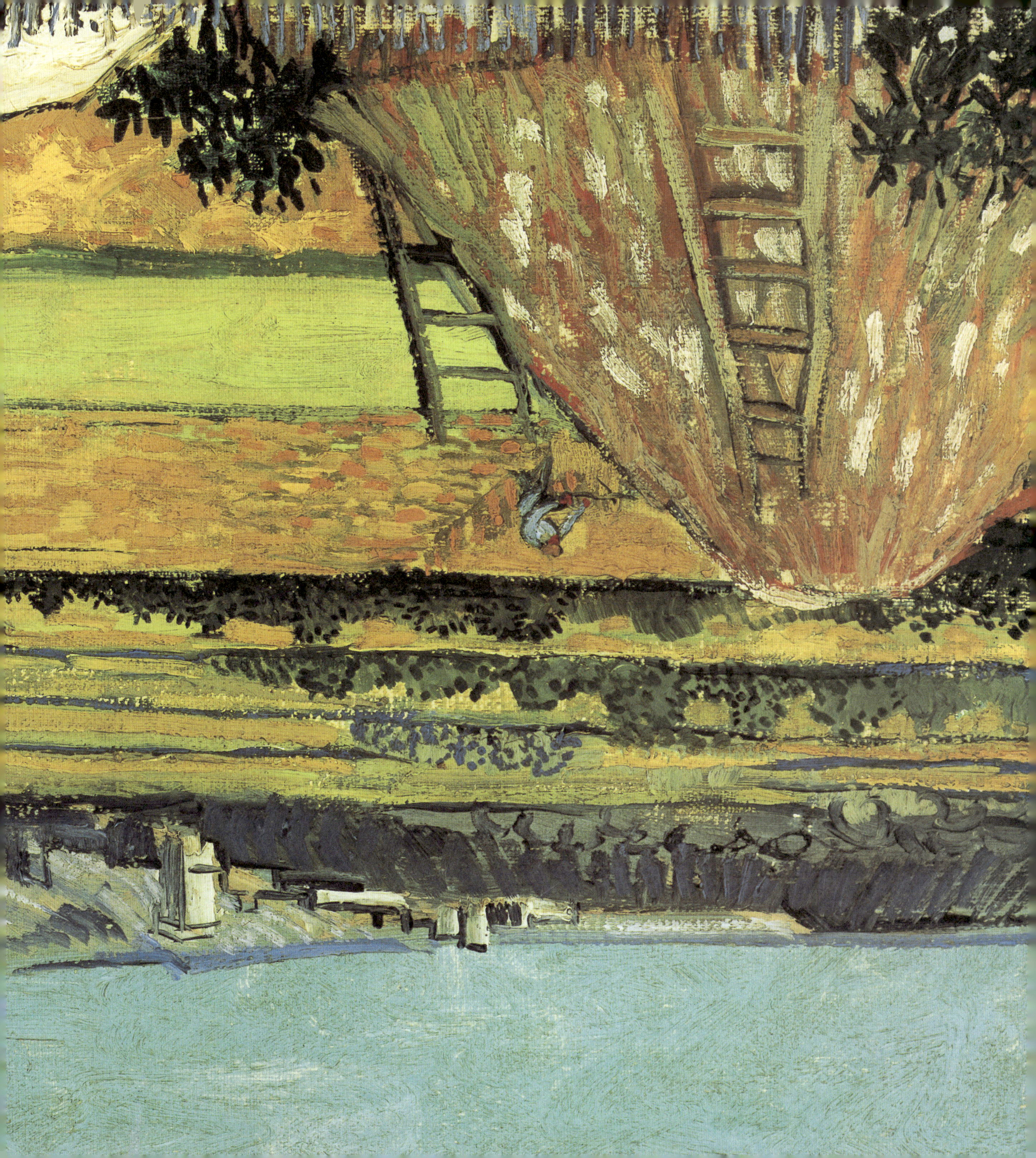

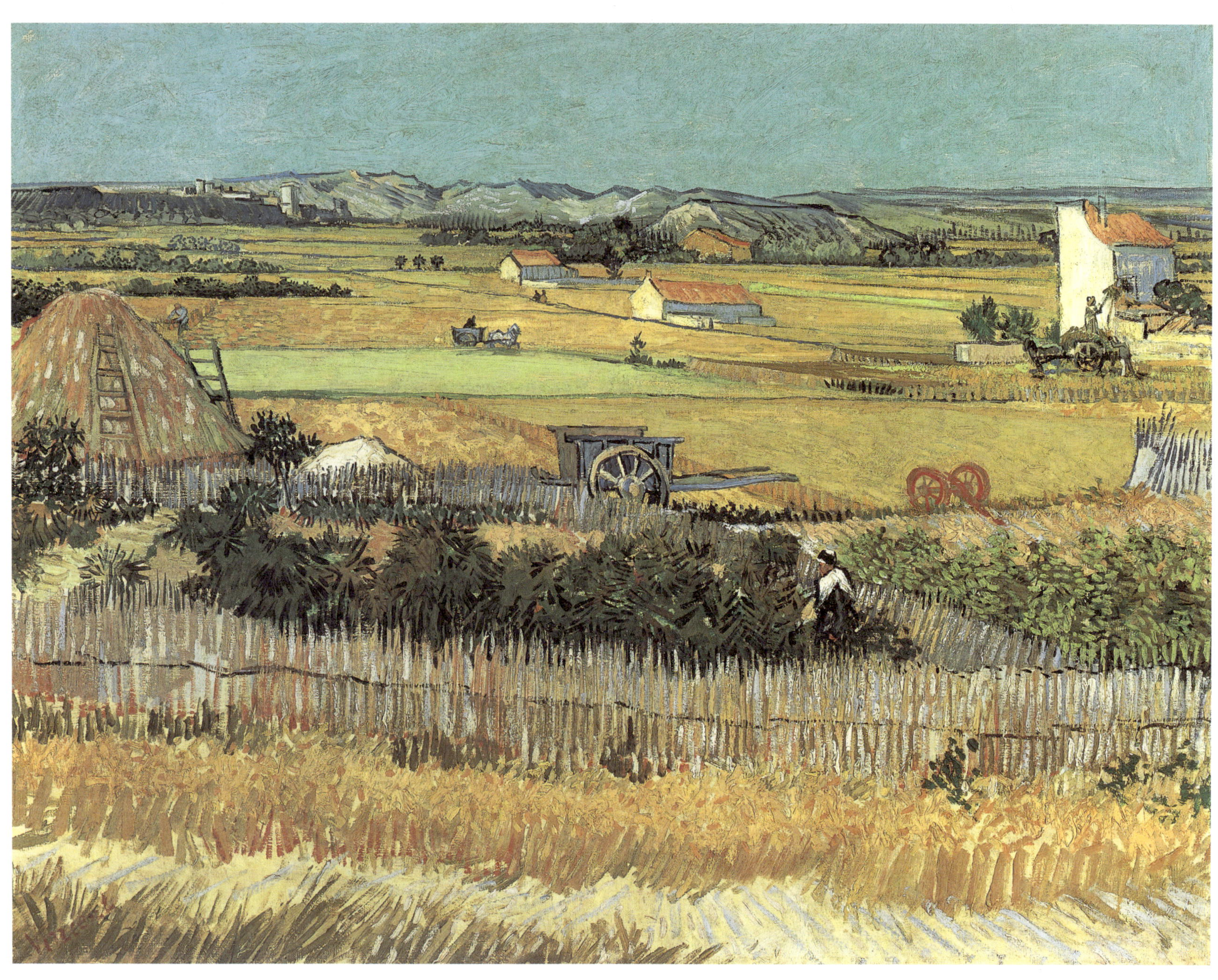

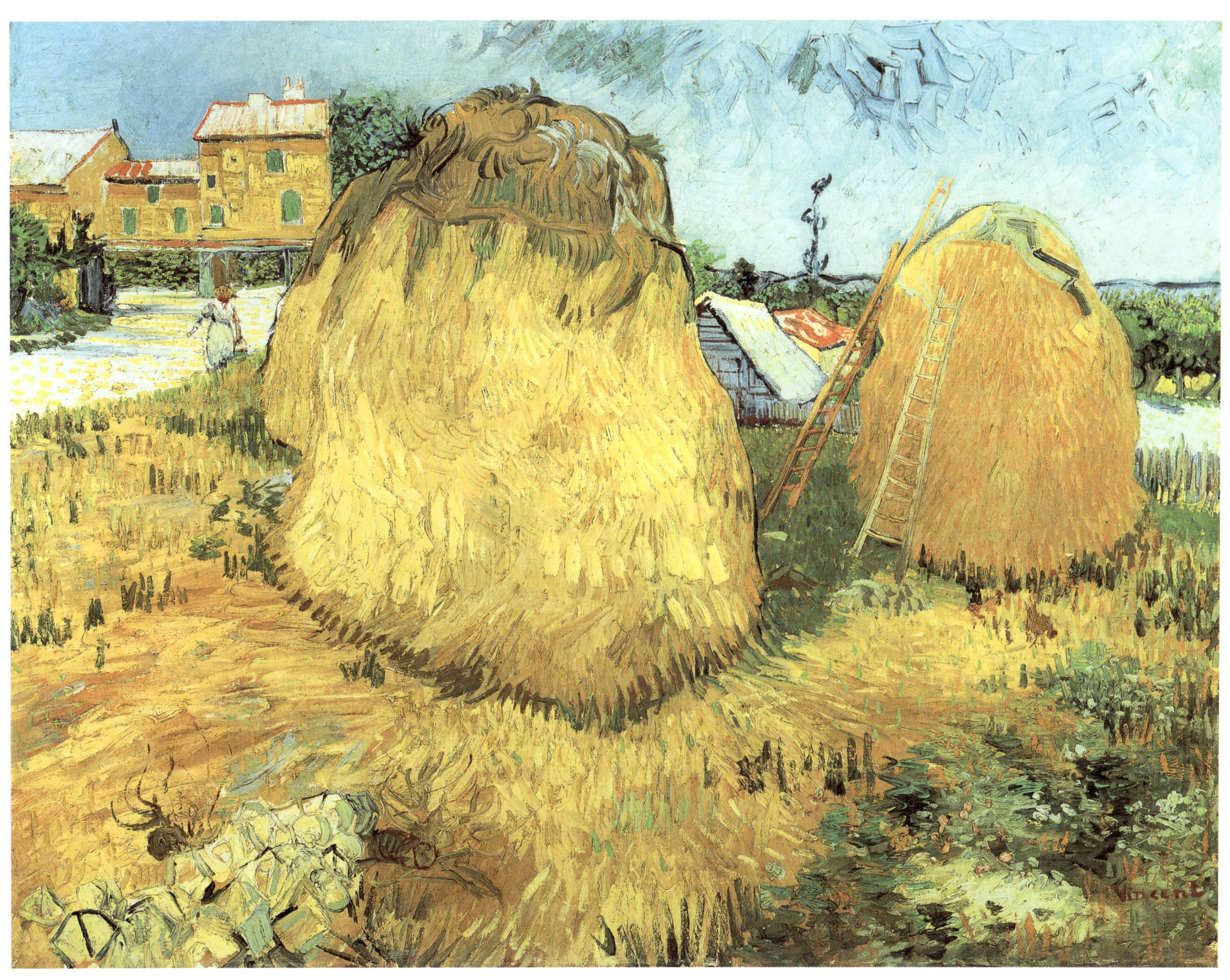
Vincent

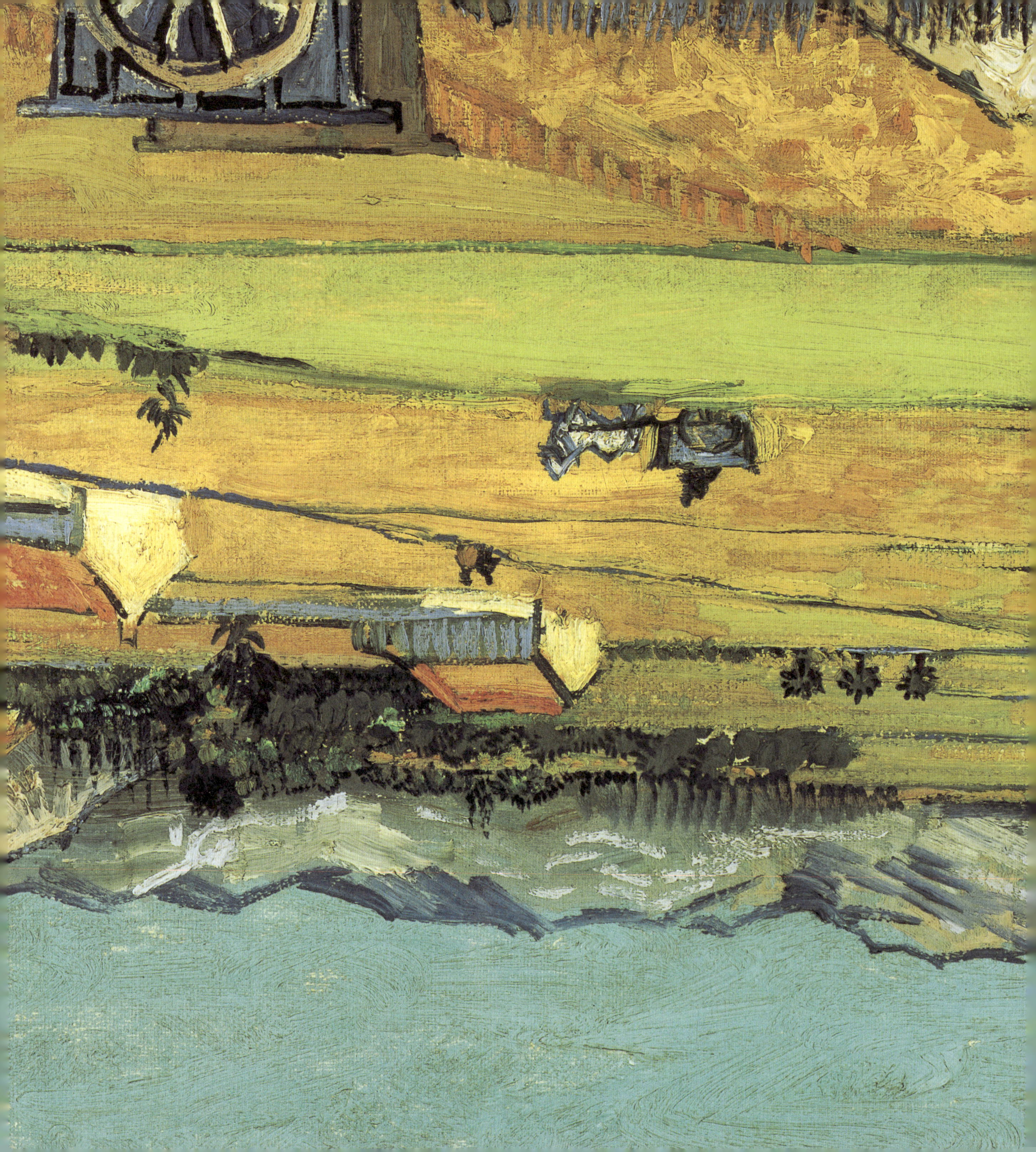

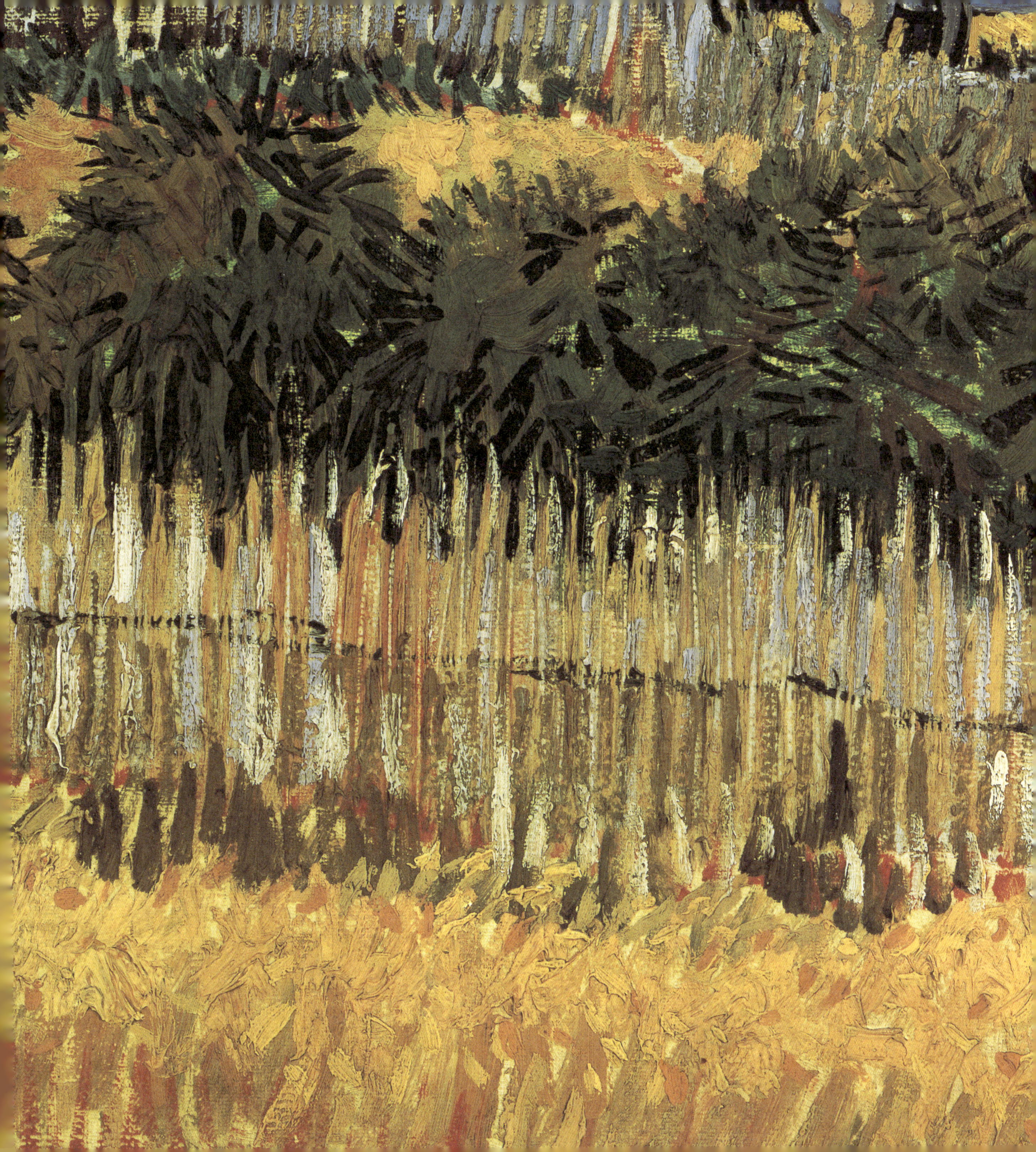

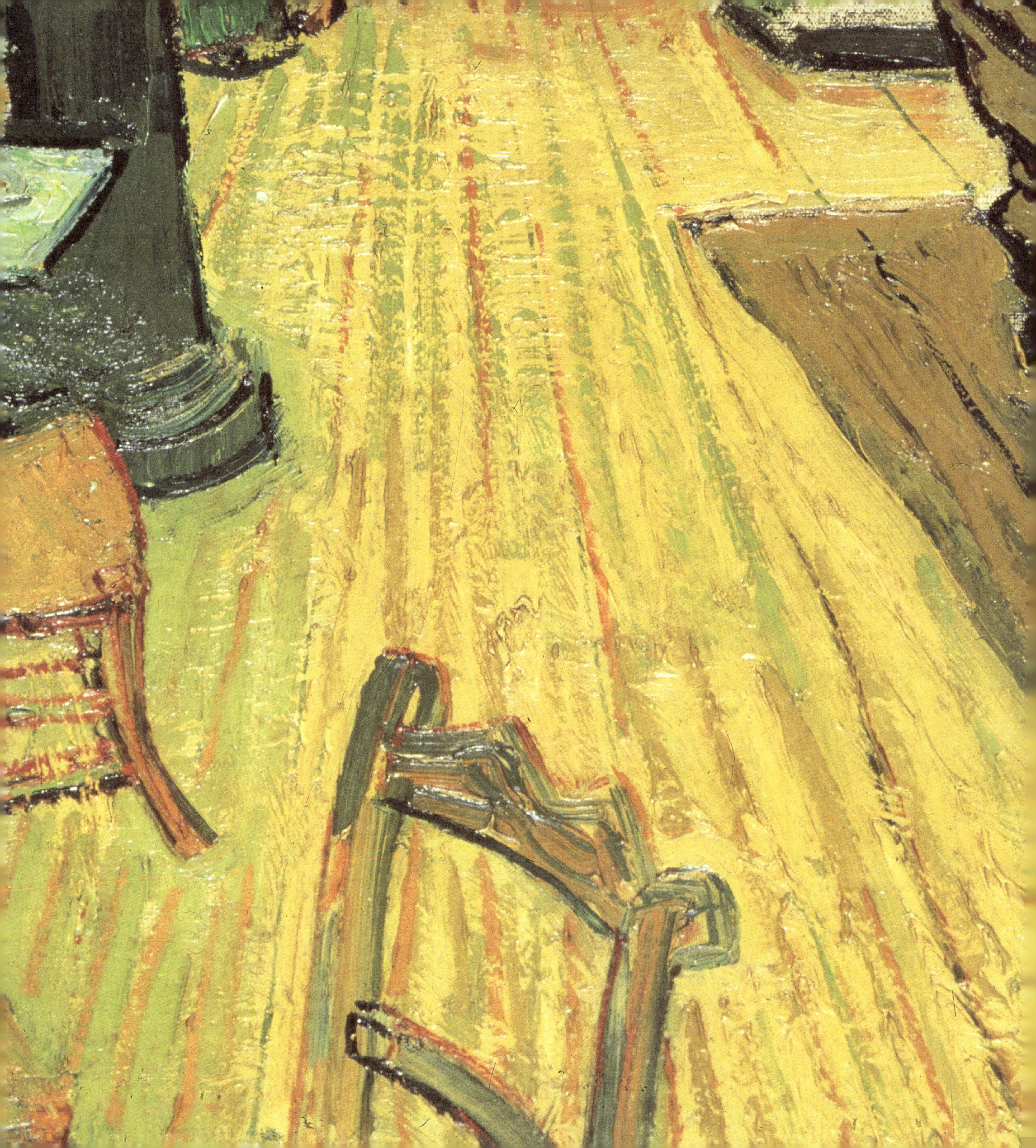

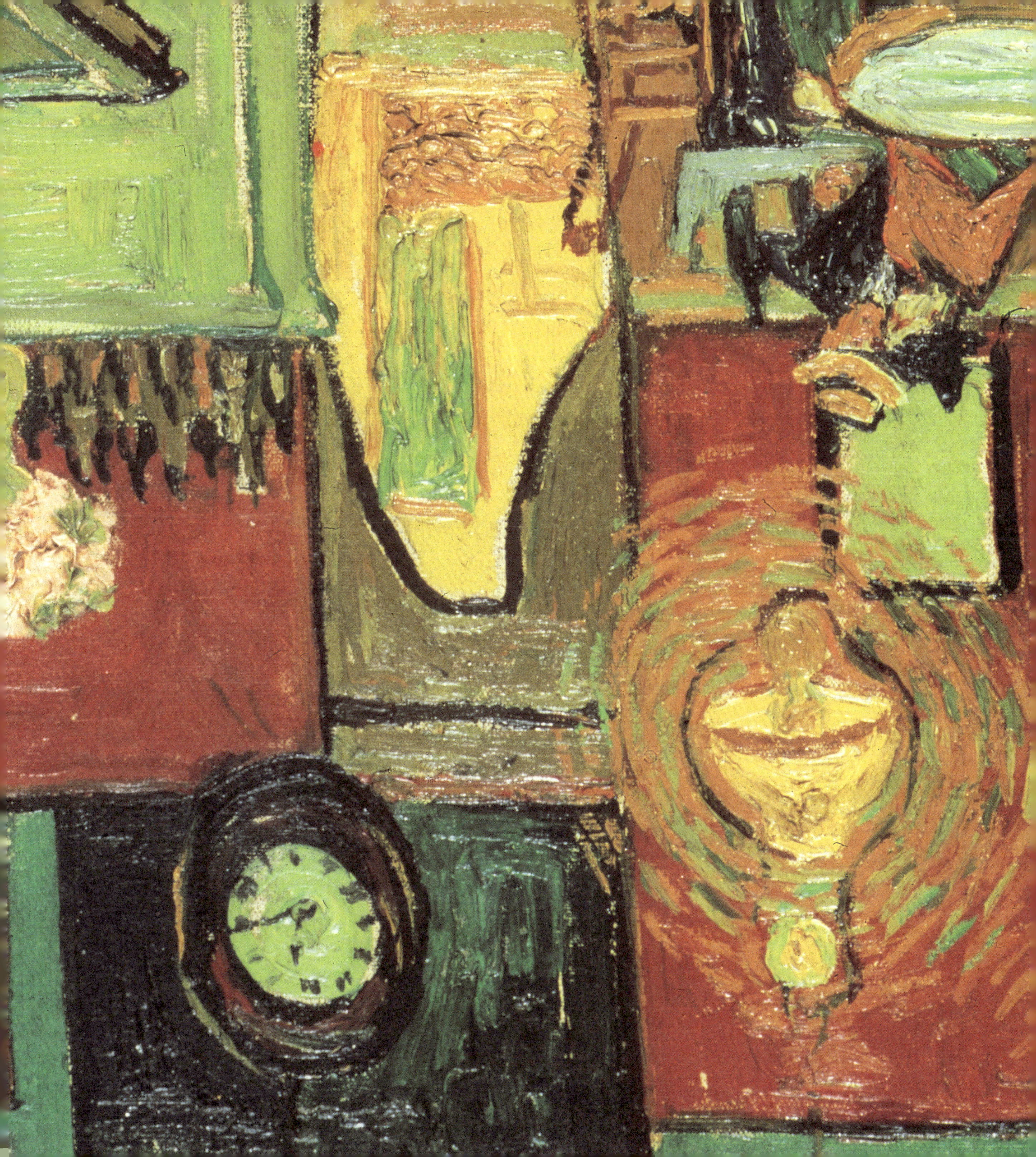

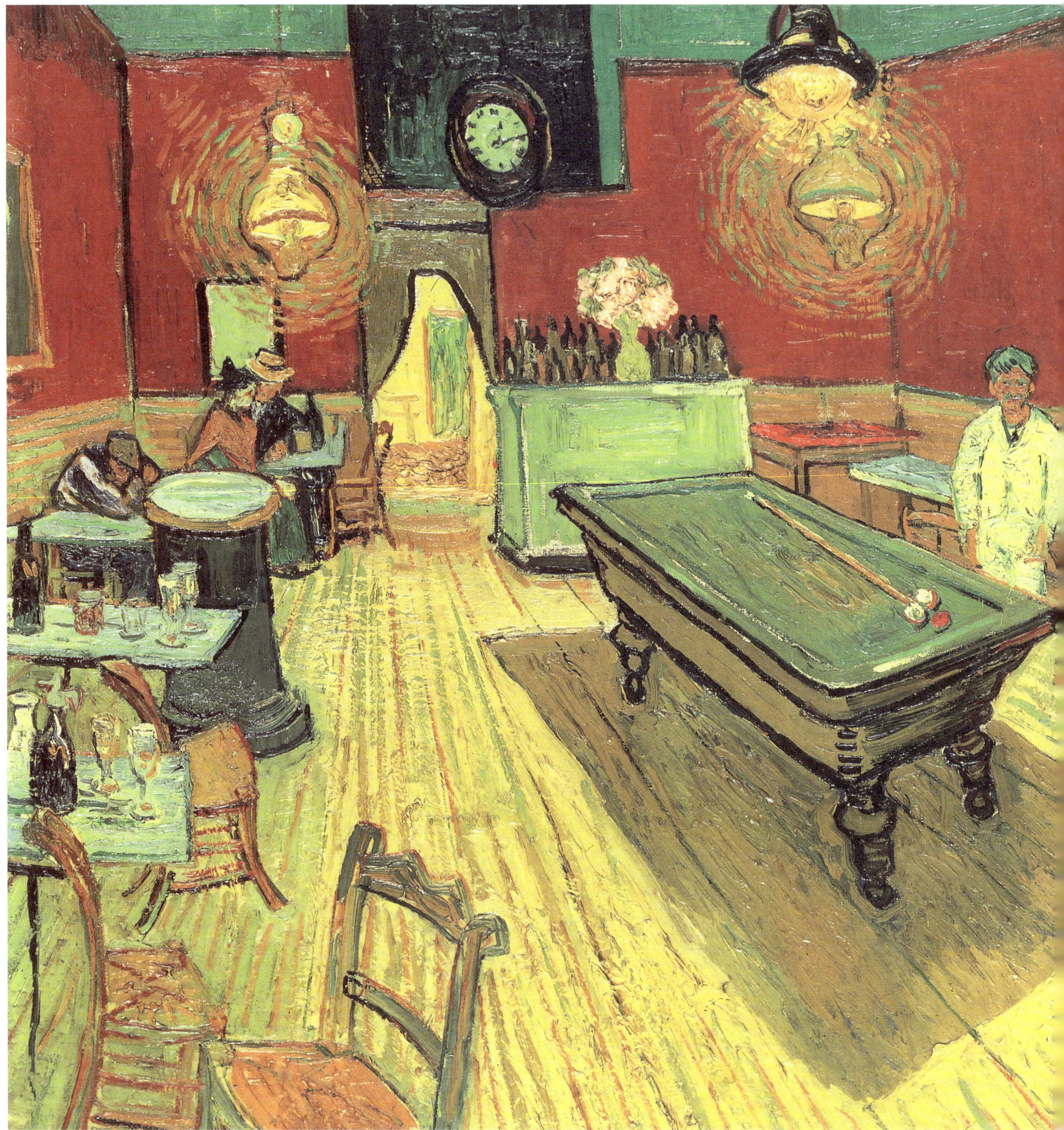

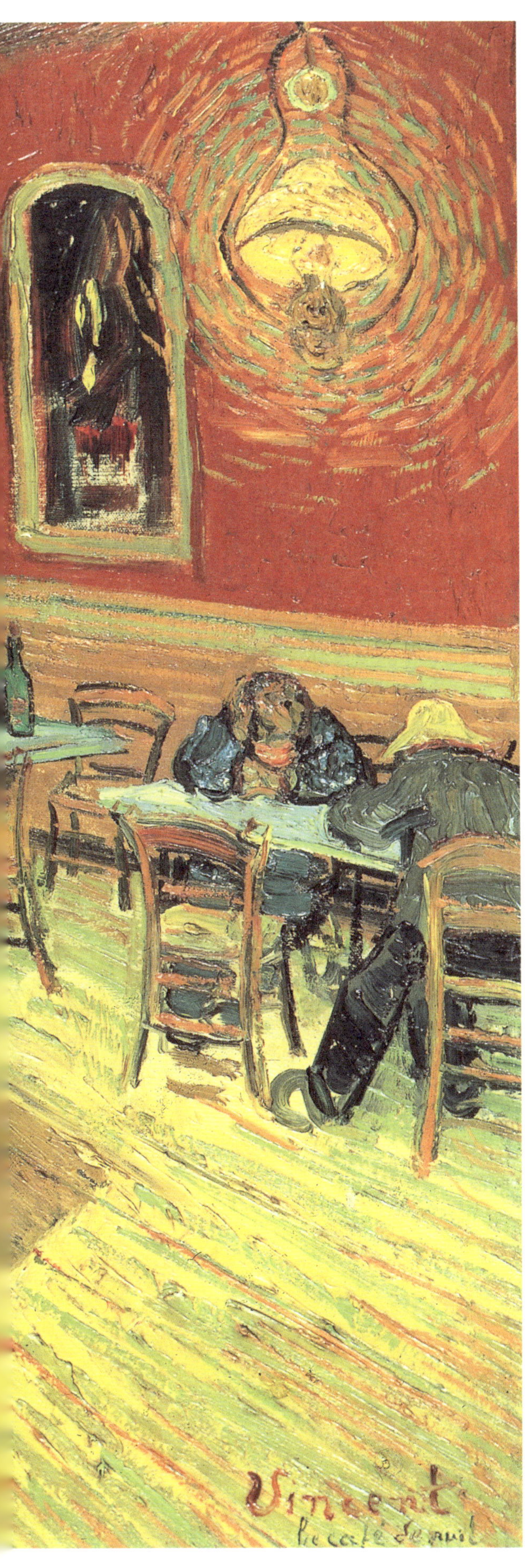
Vincent
le café de nuit

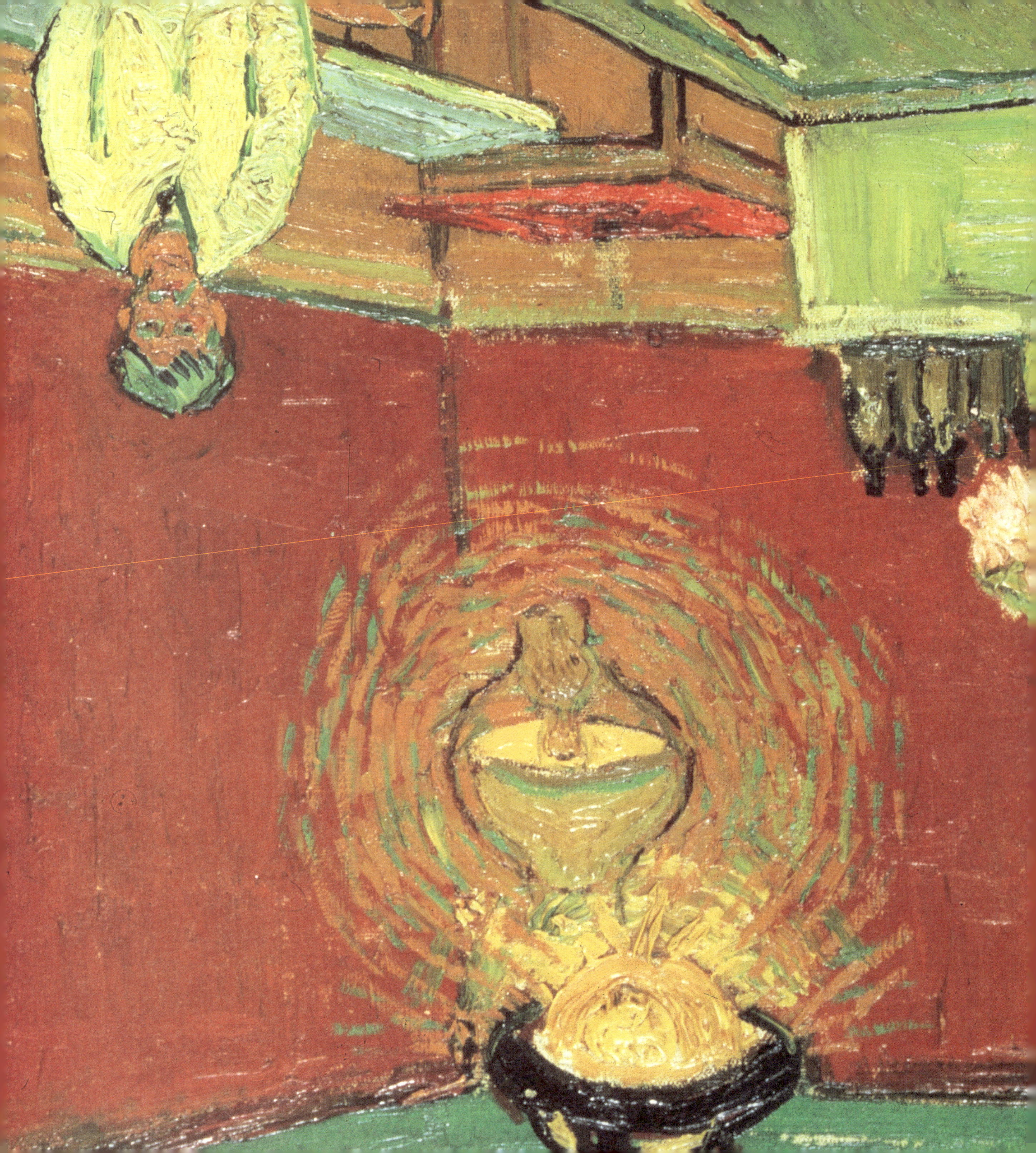

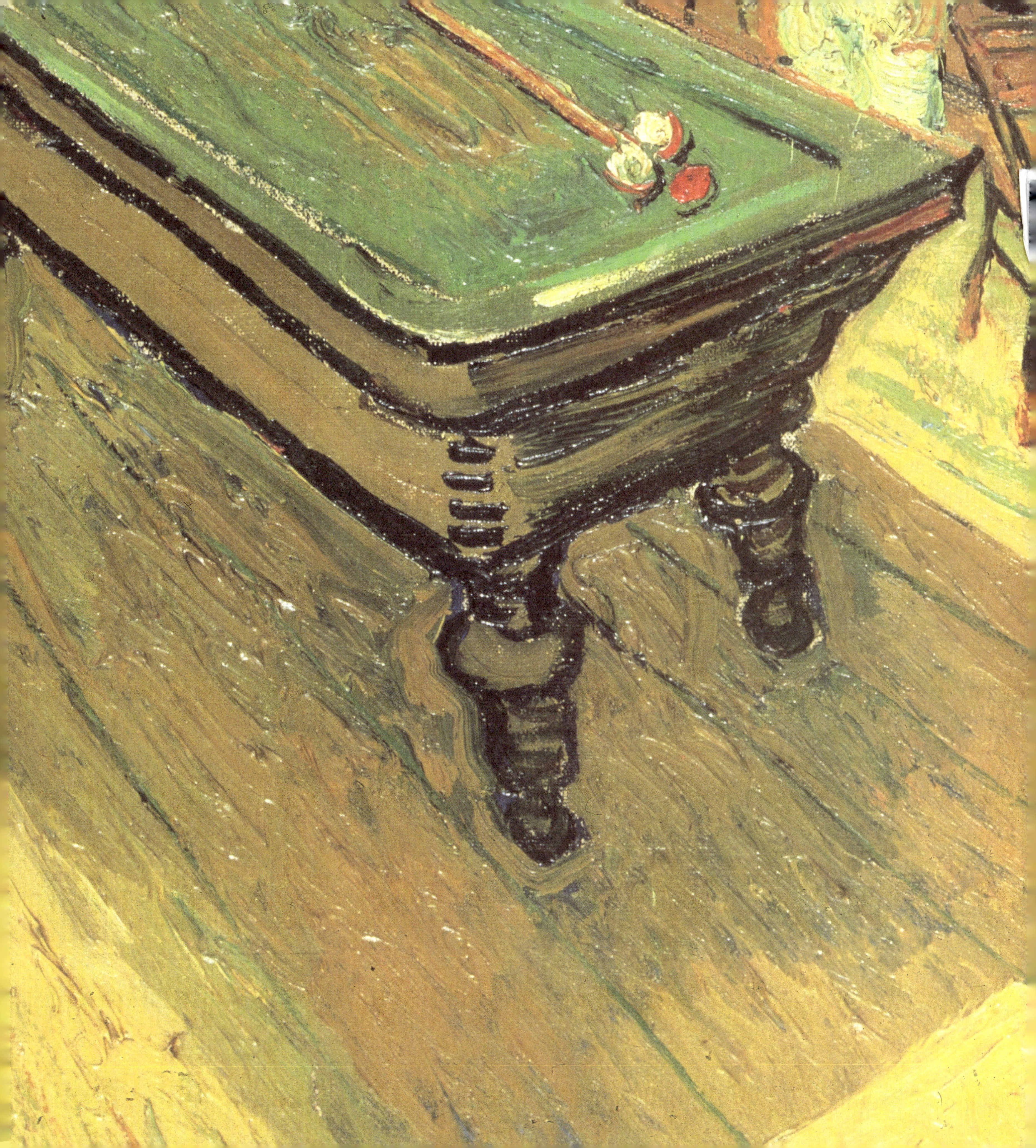

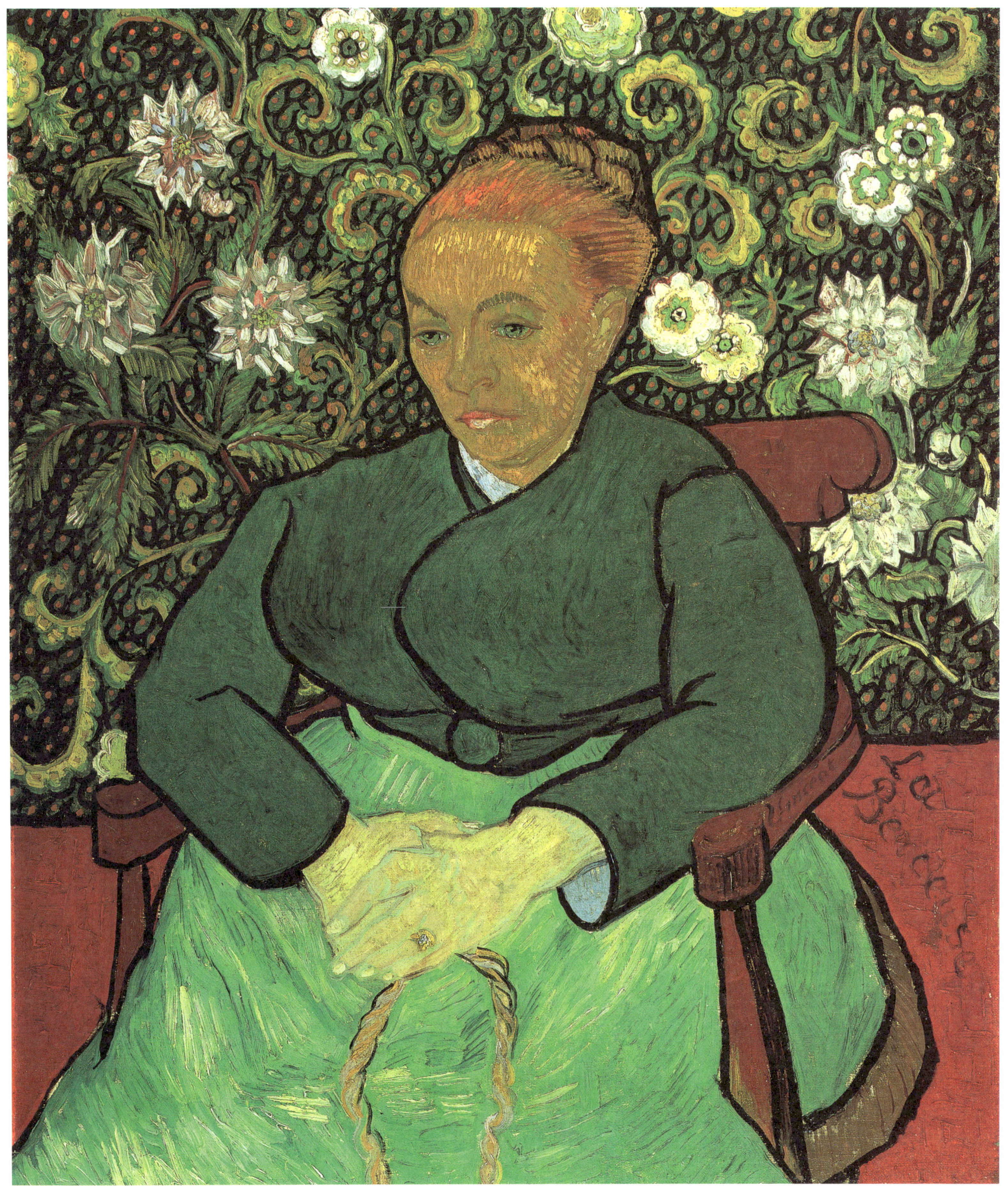
La Berceuse

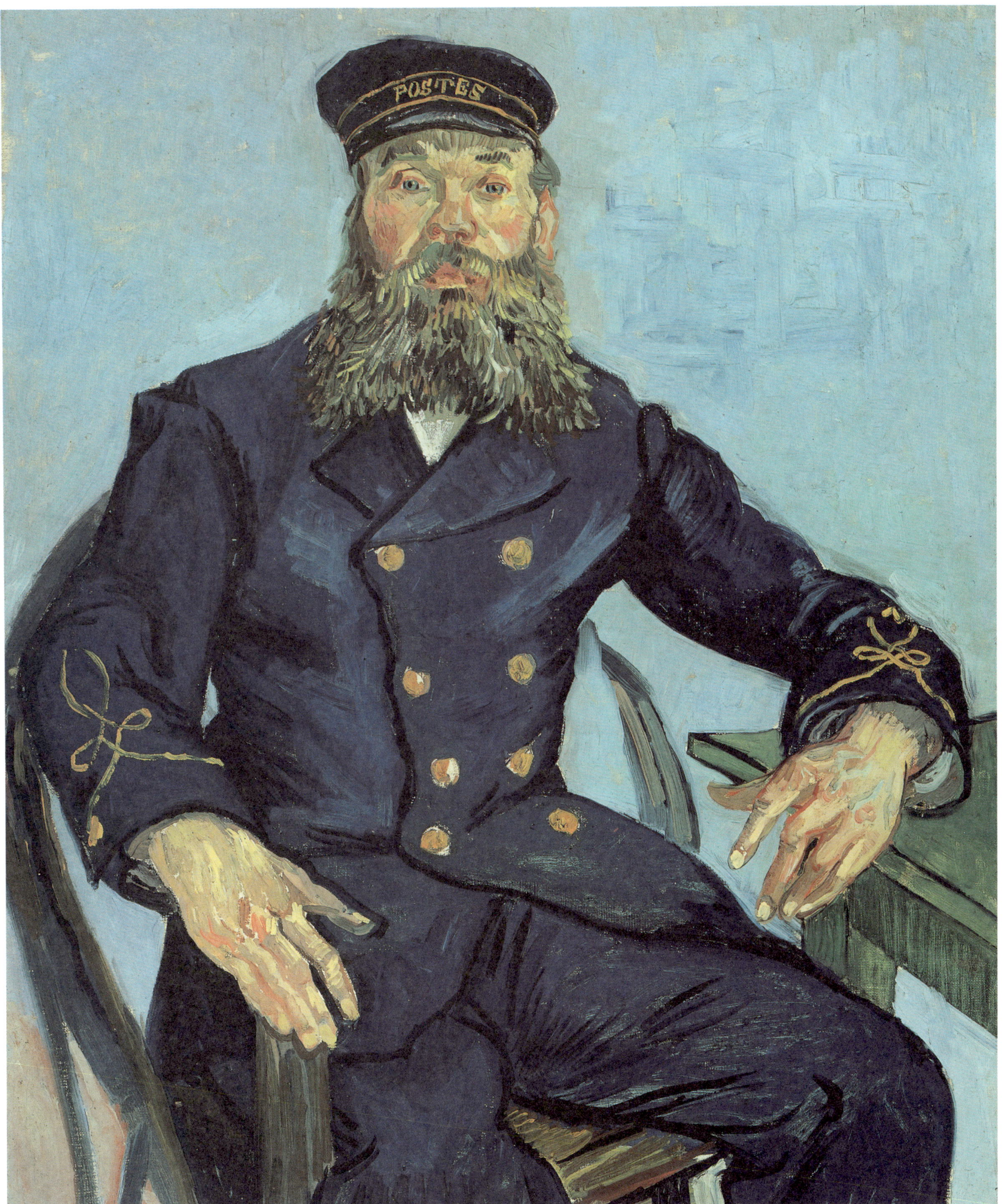
POSTES

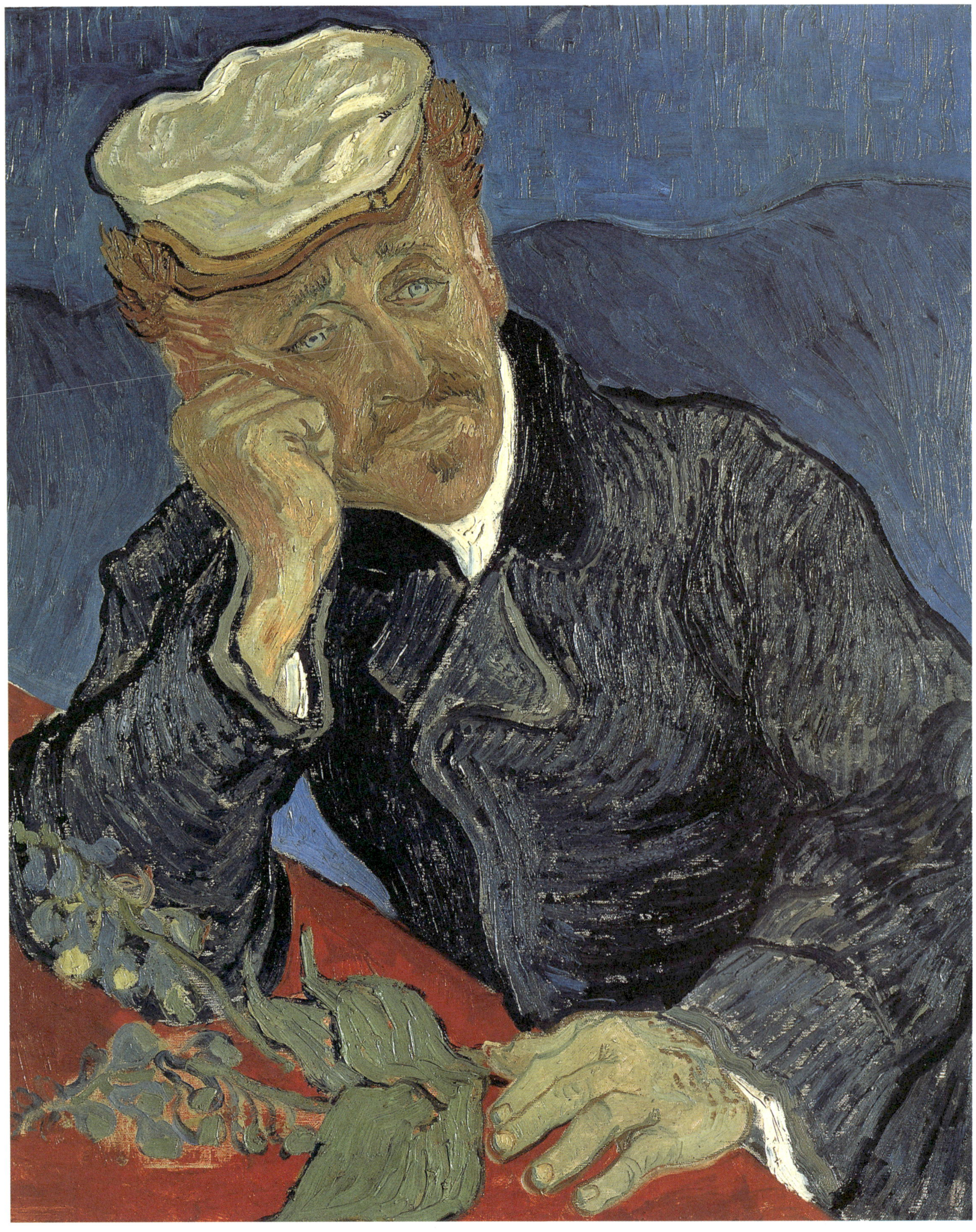

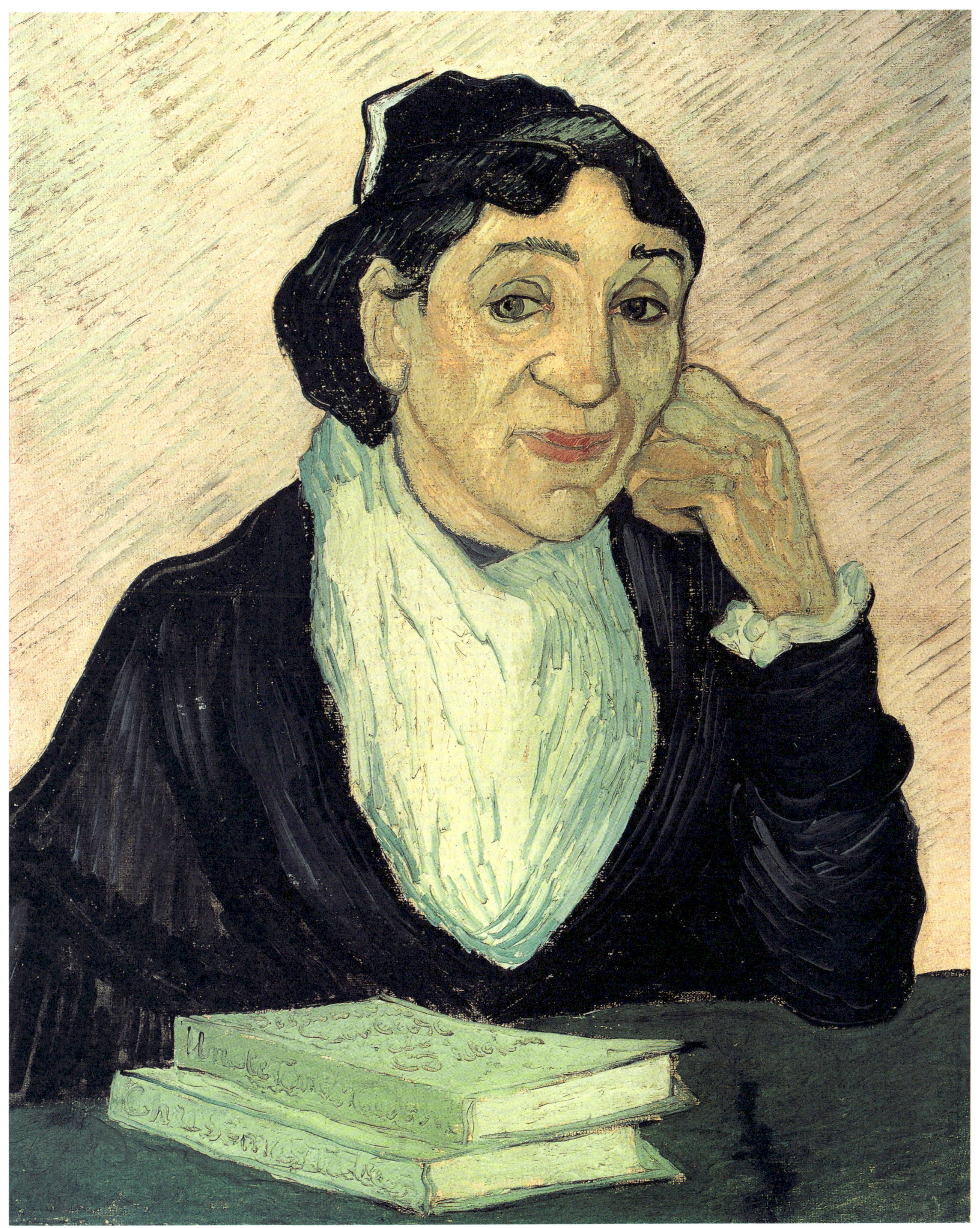

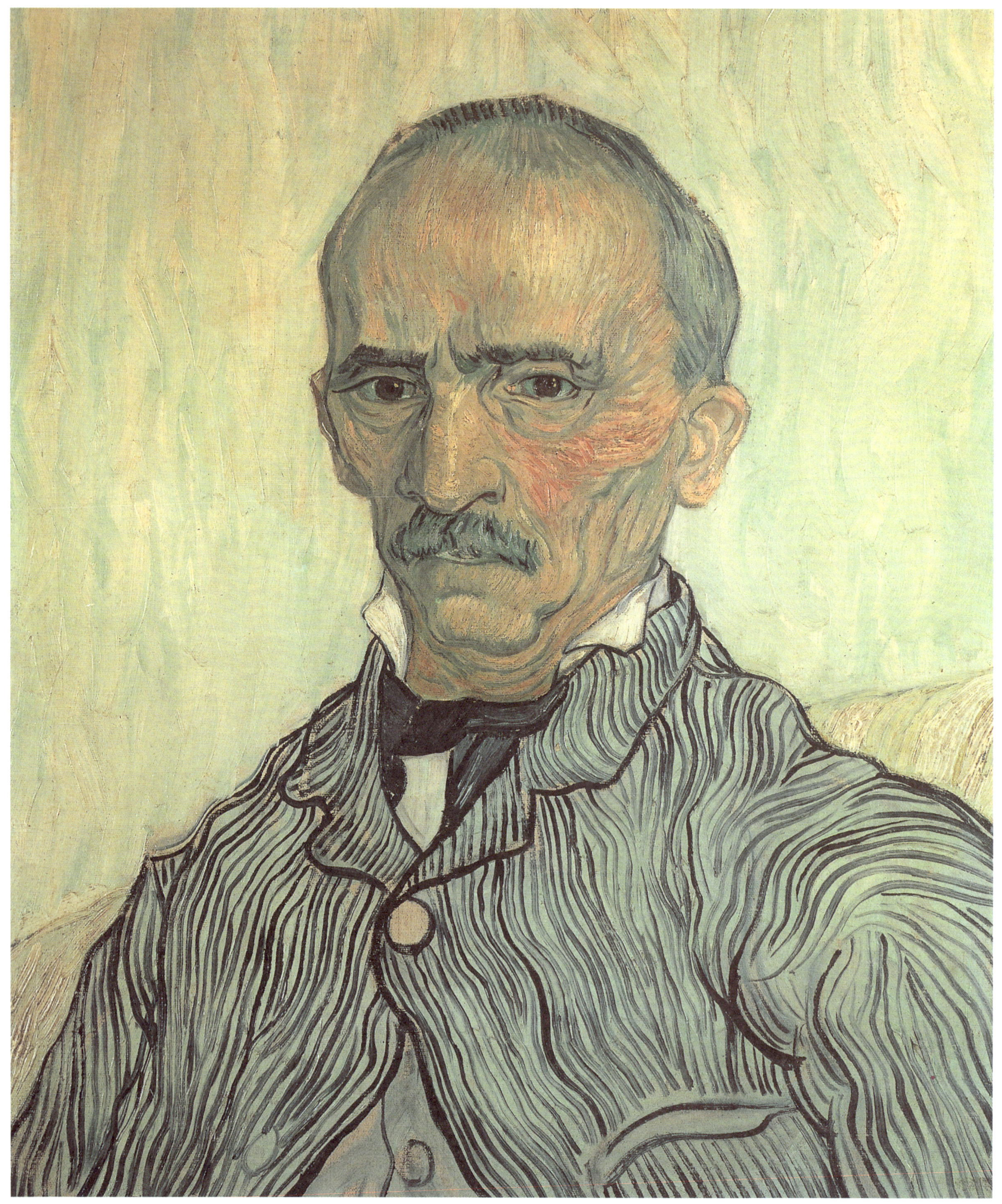

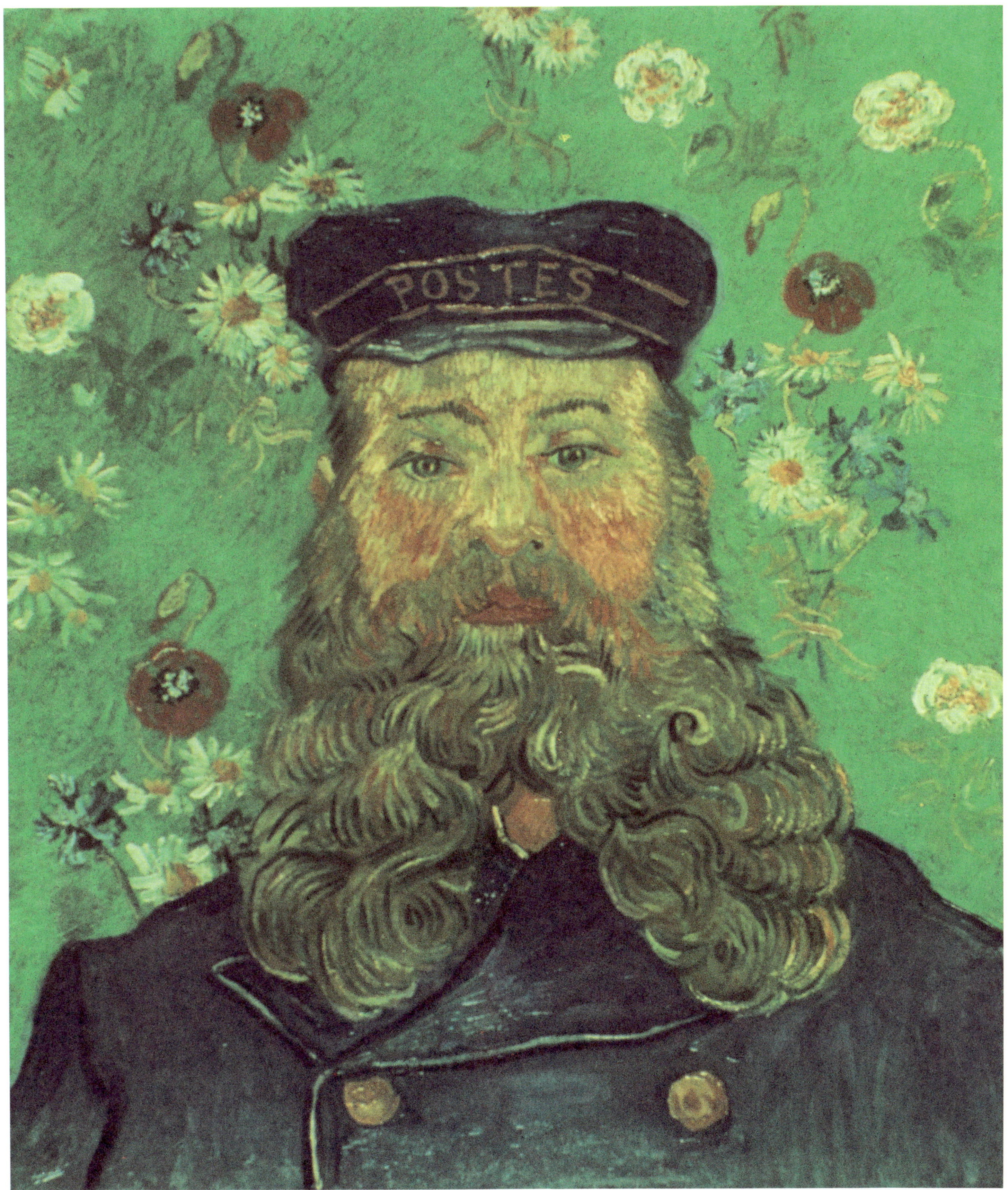
POSTES

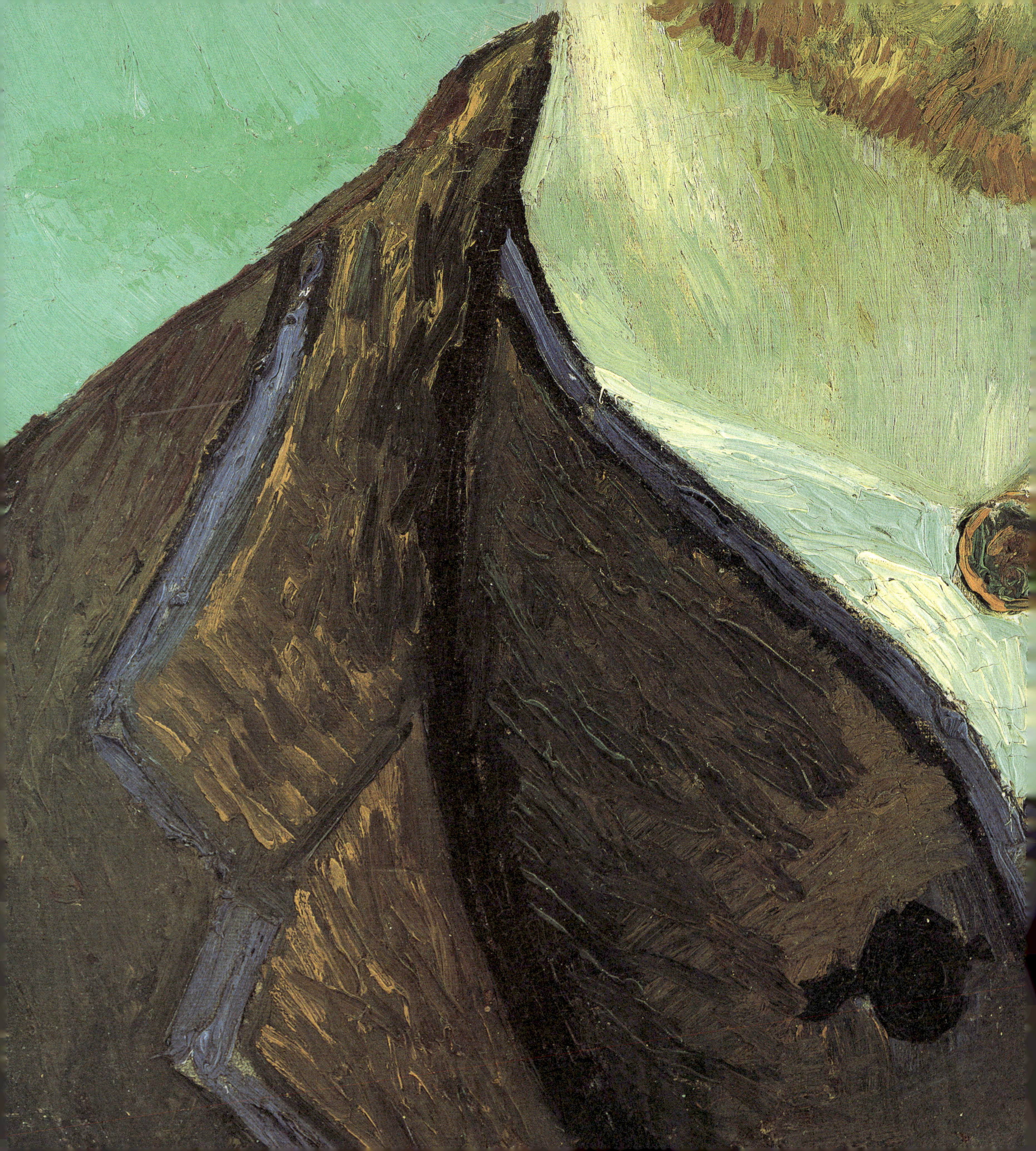

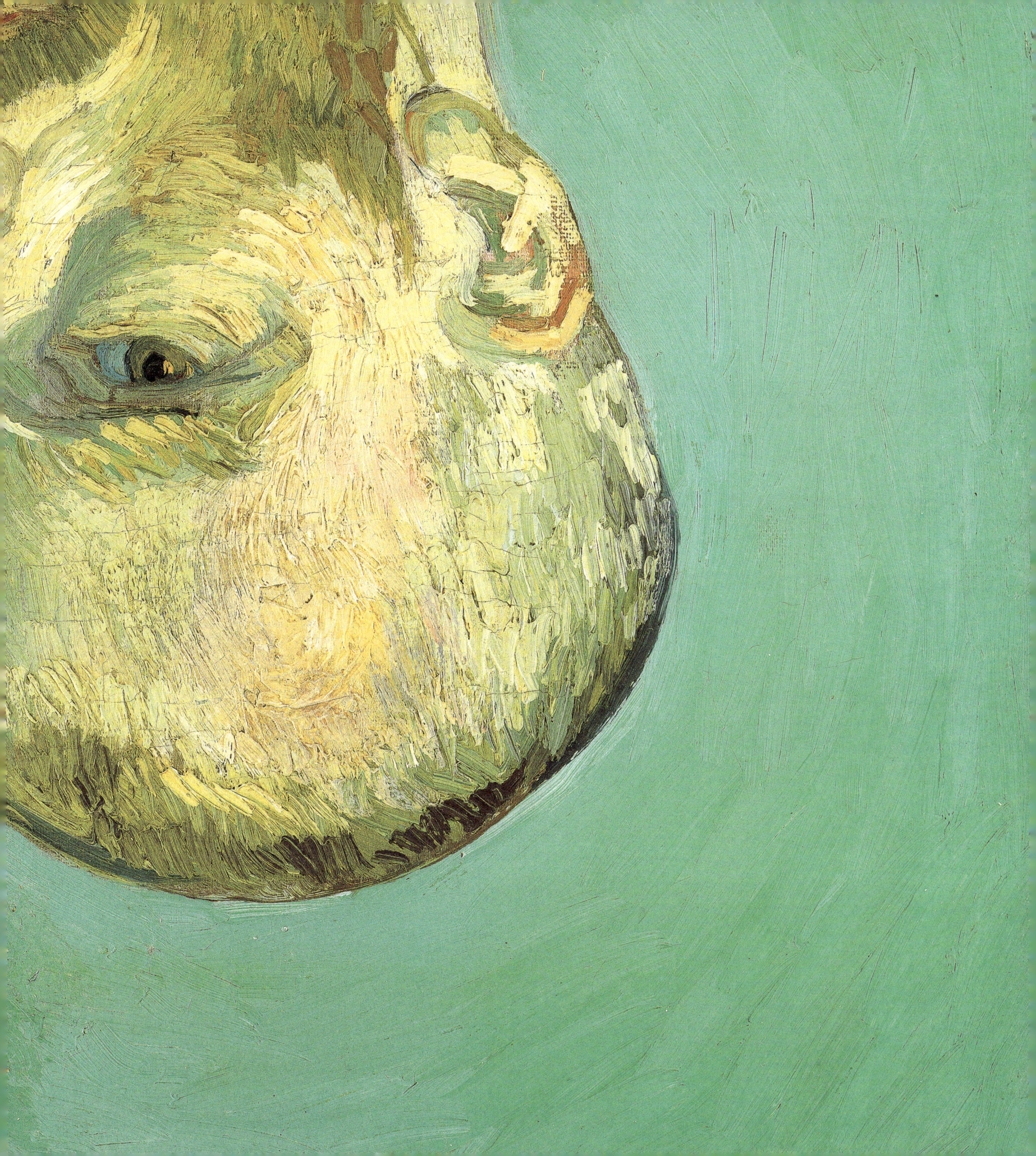

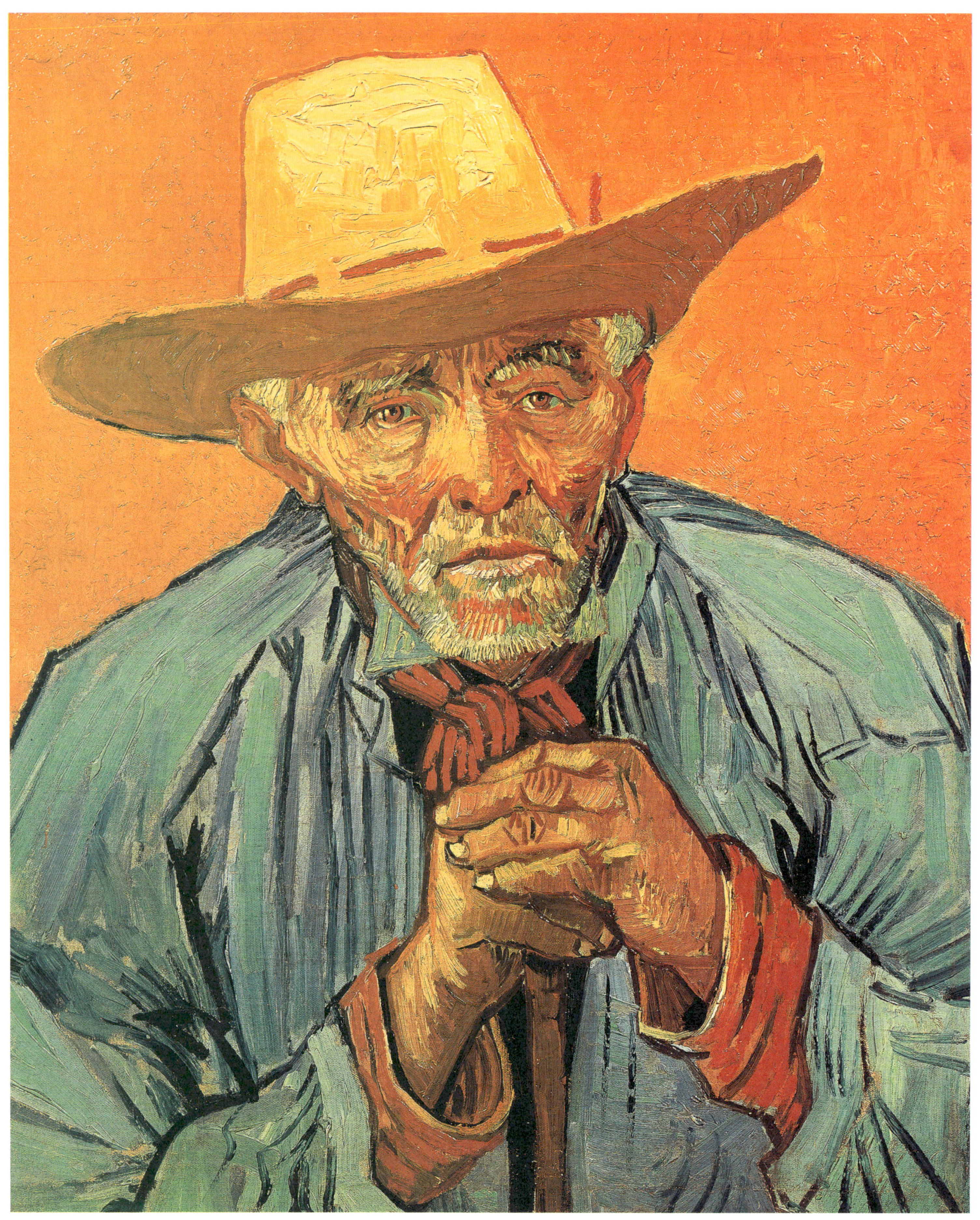

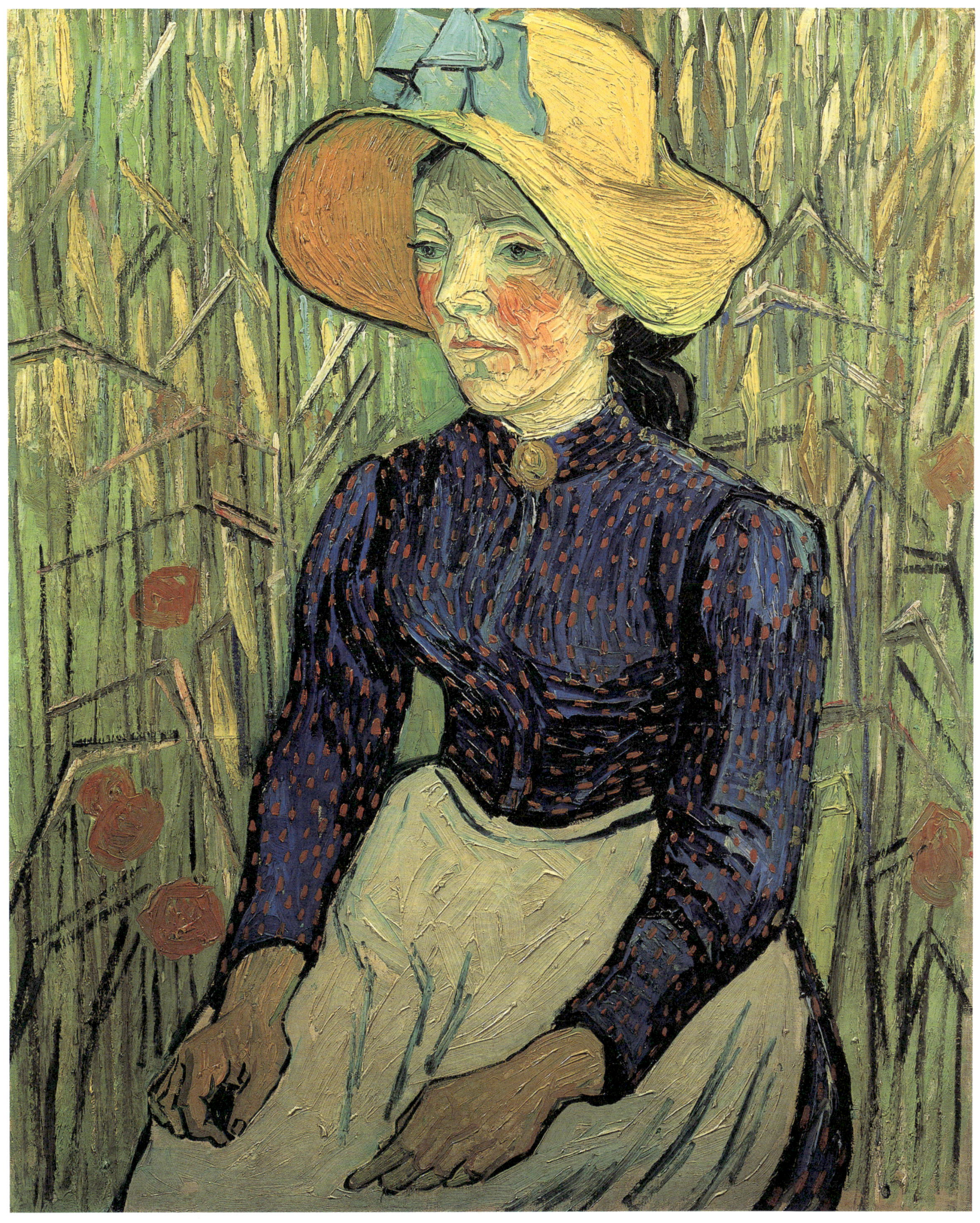

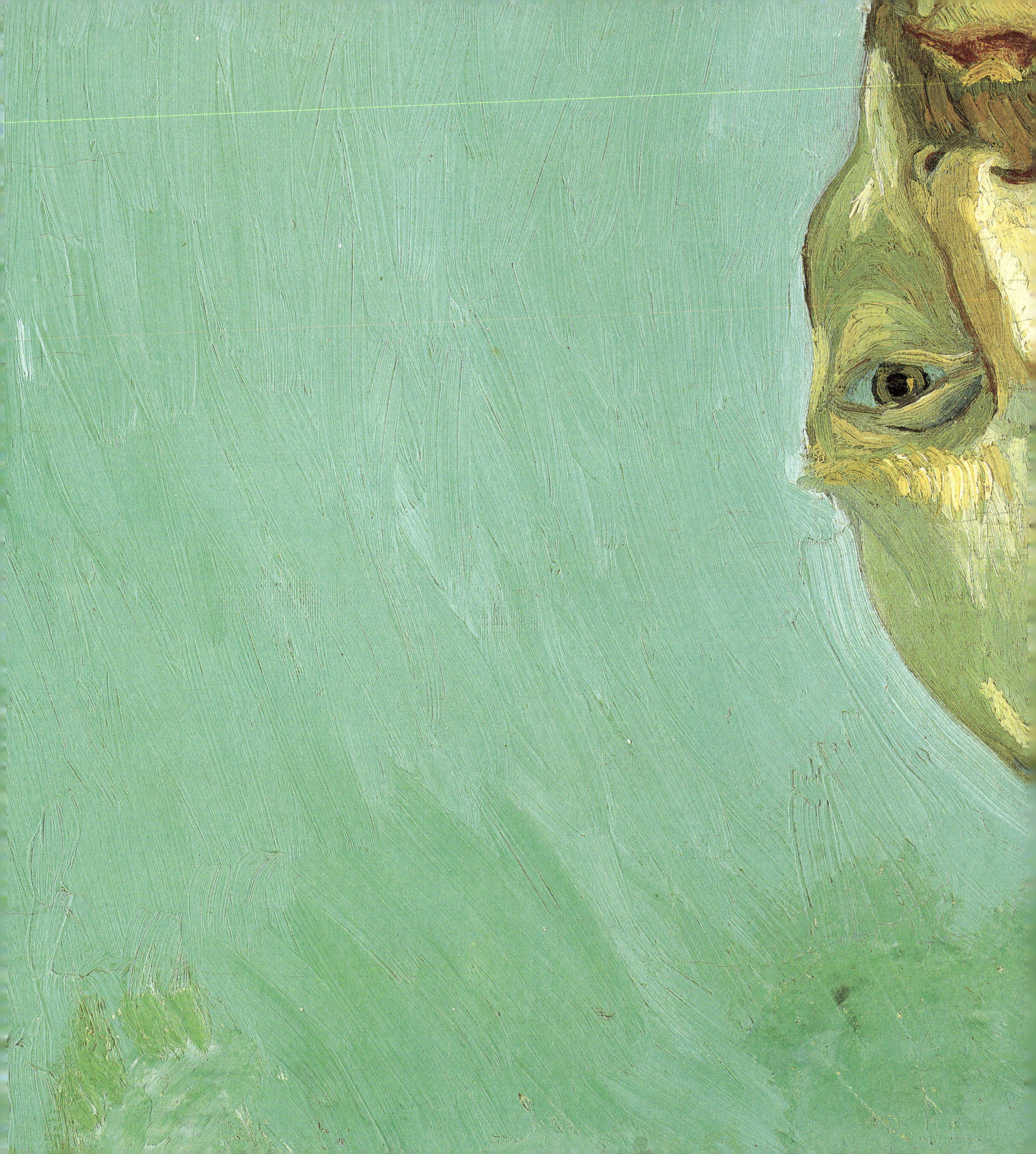

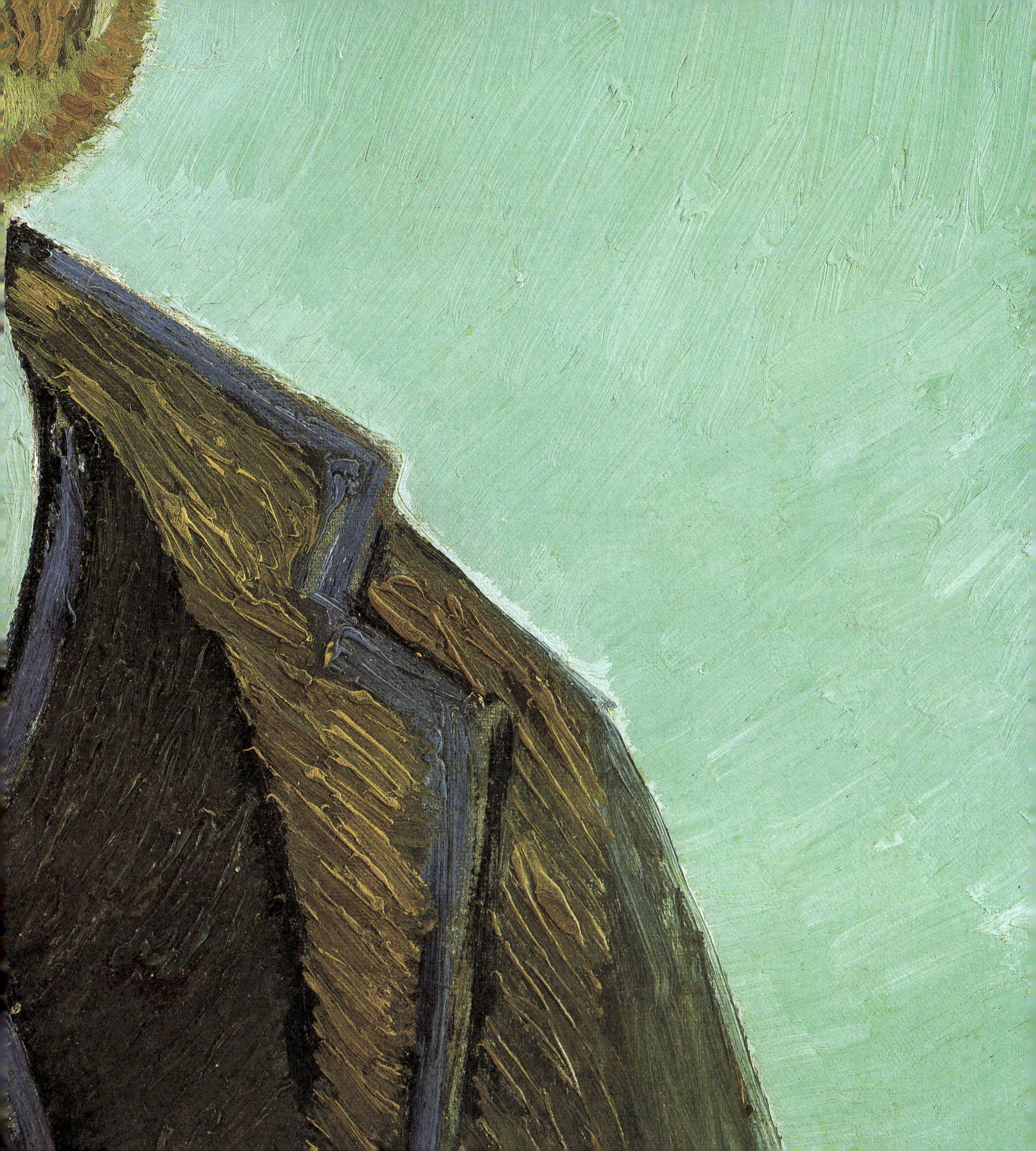

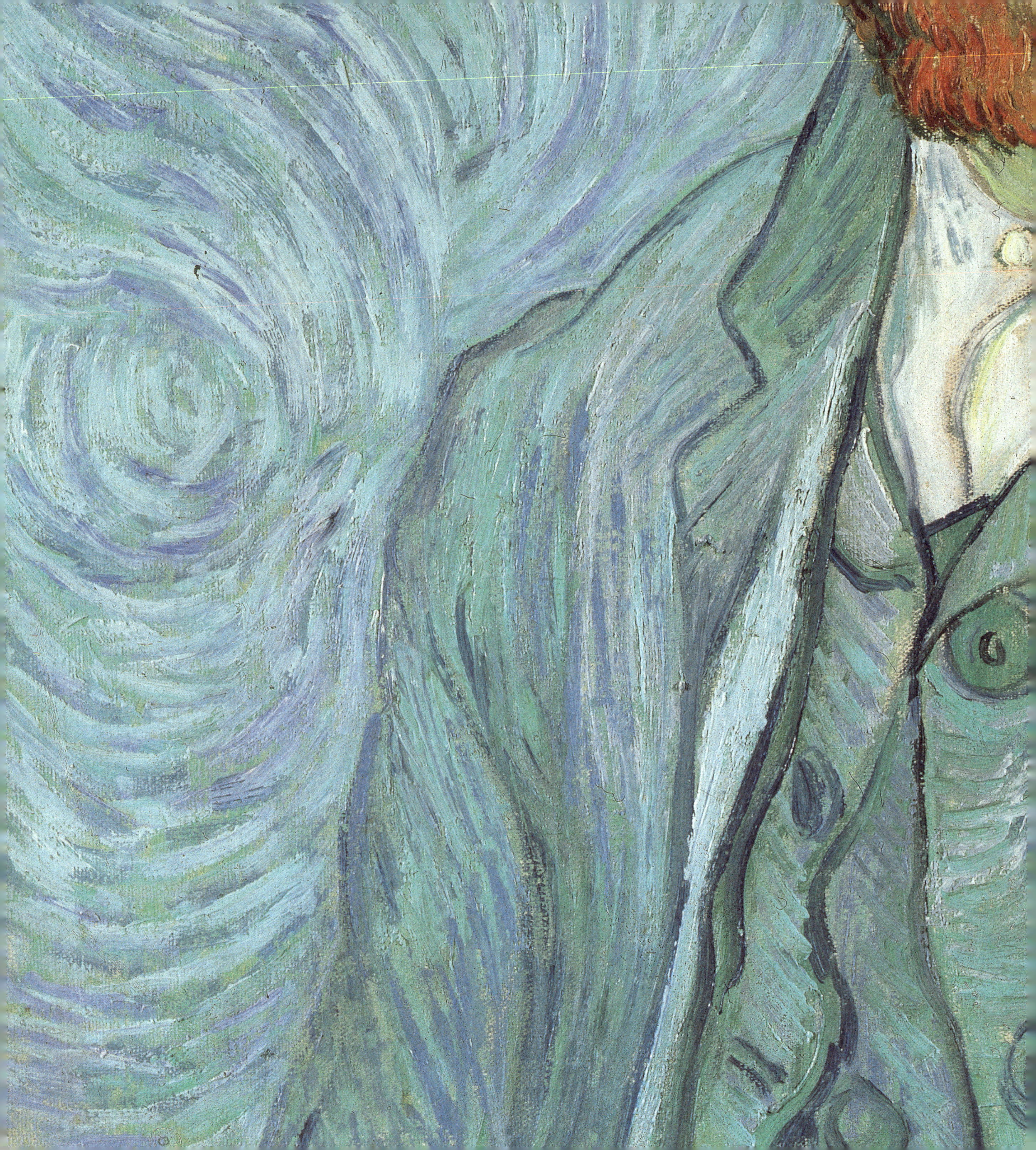

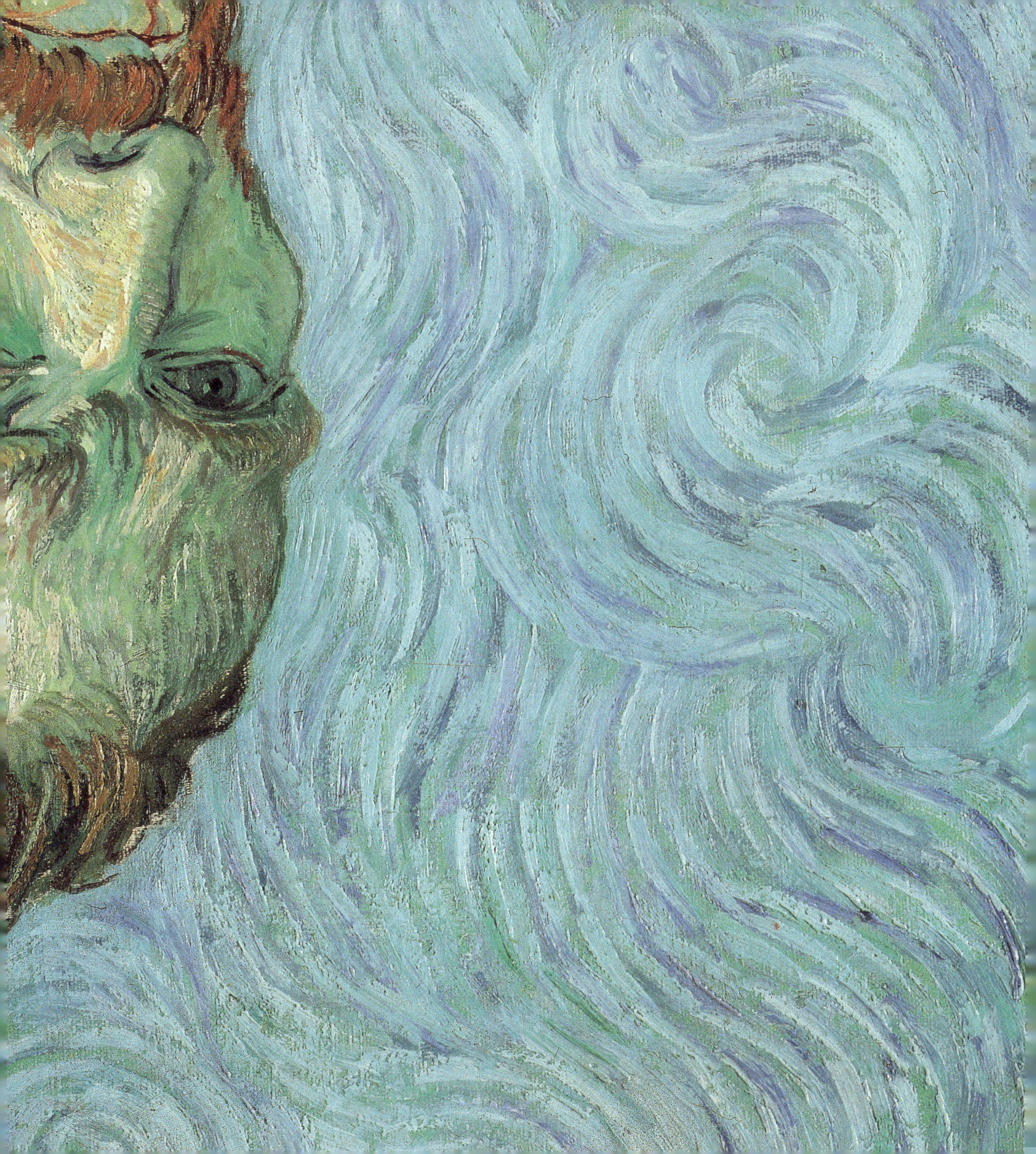

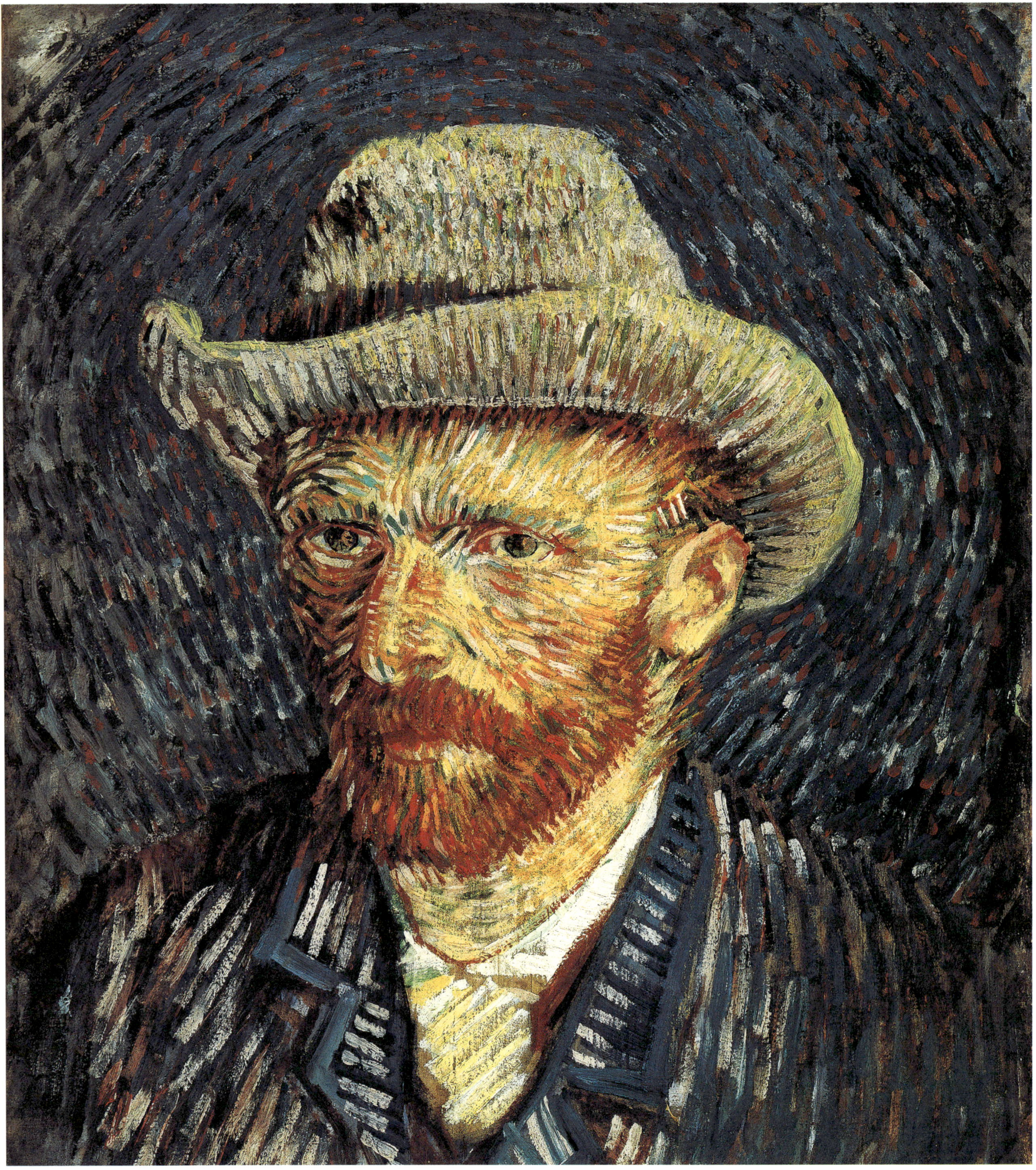

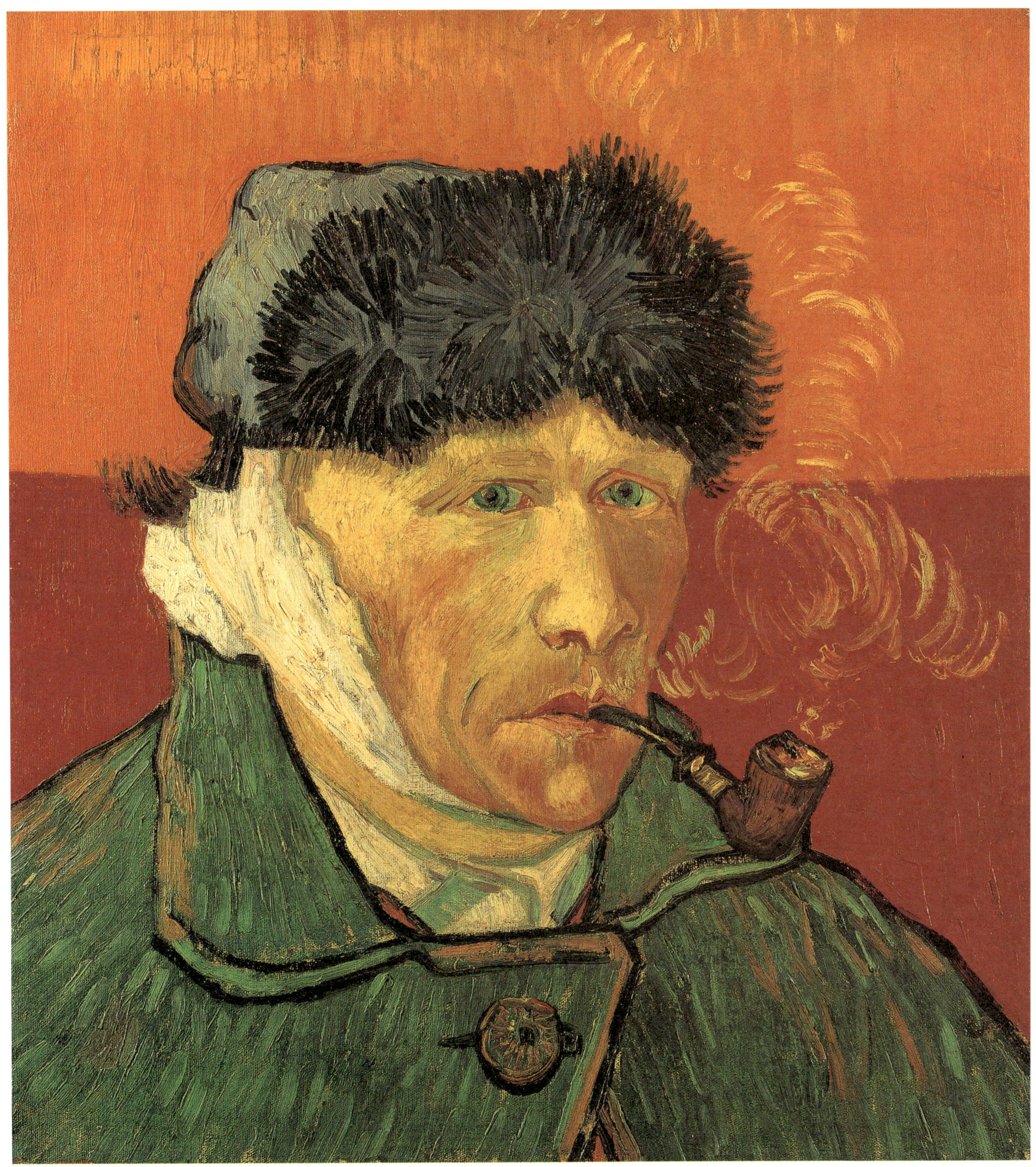

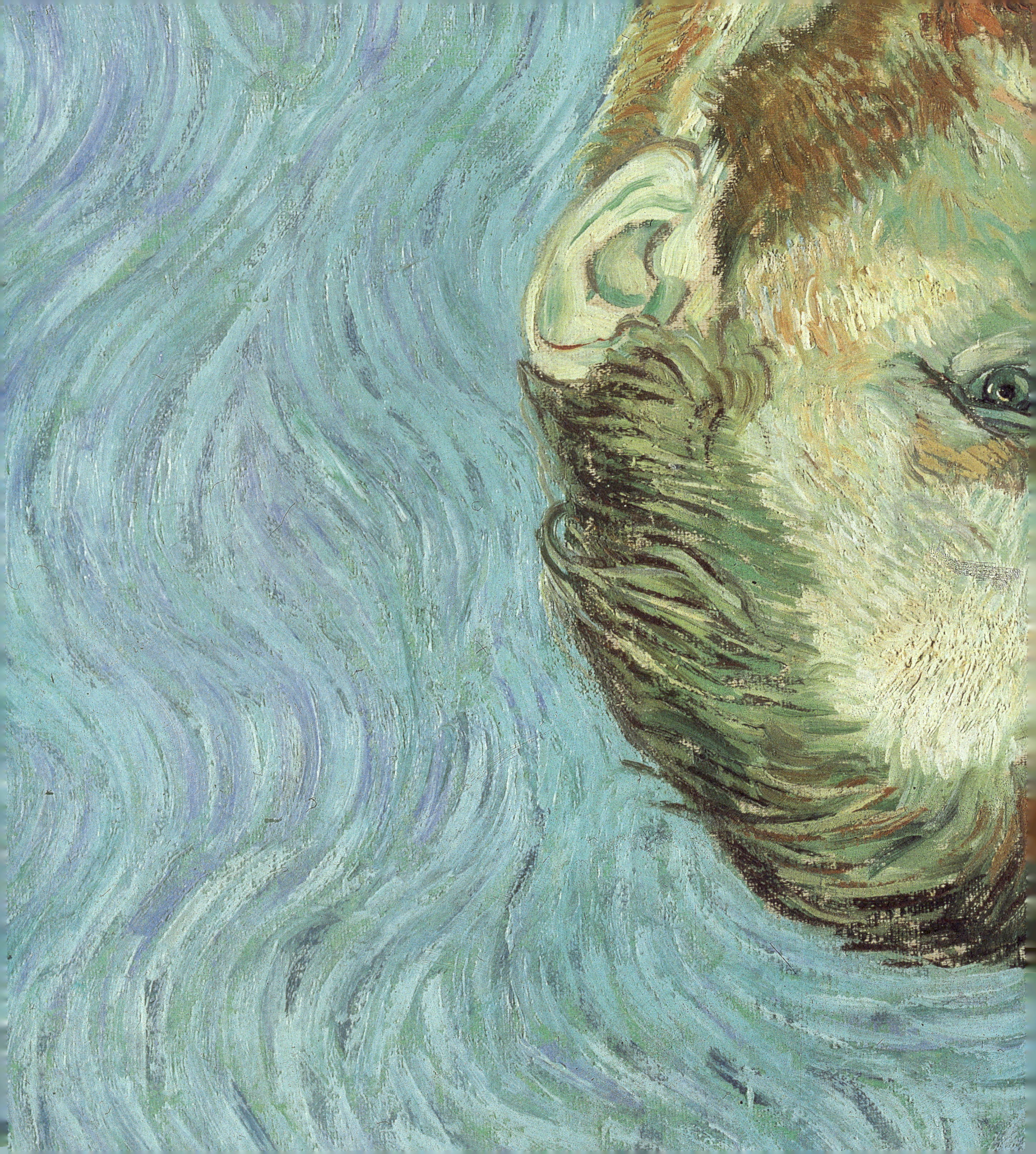

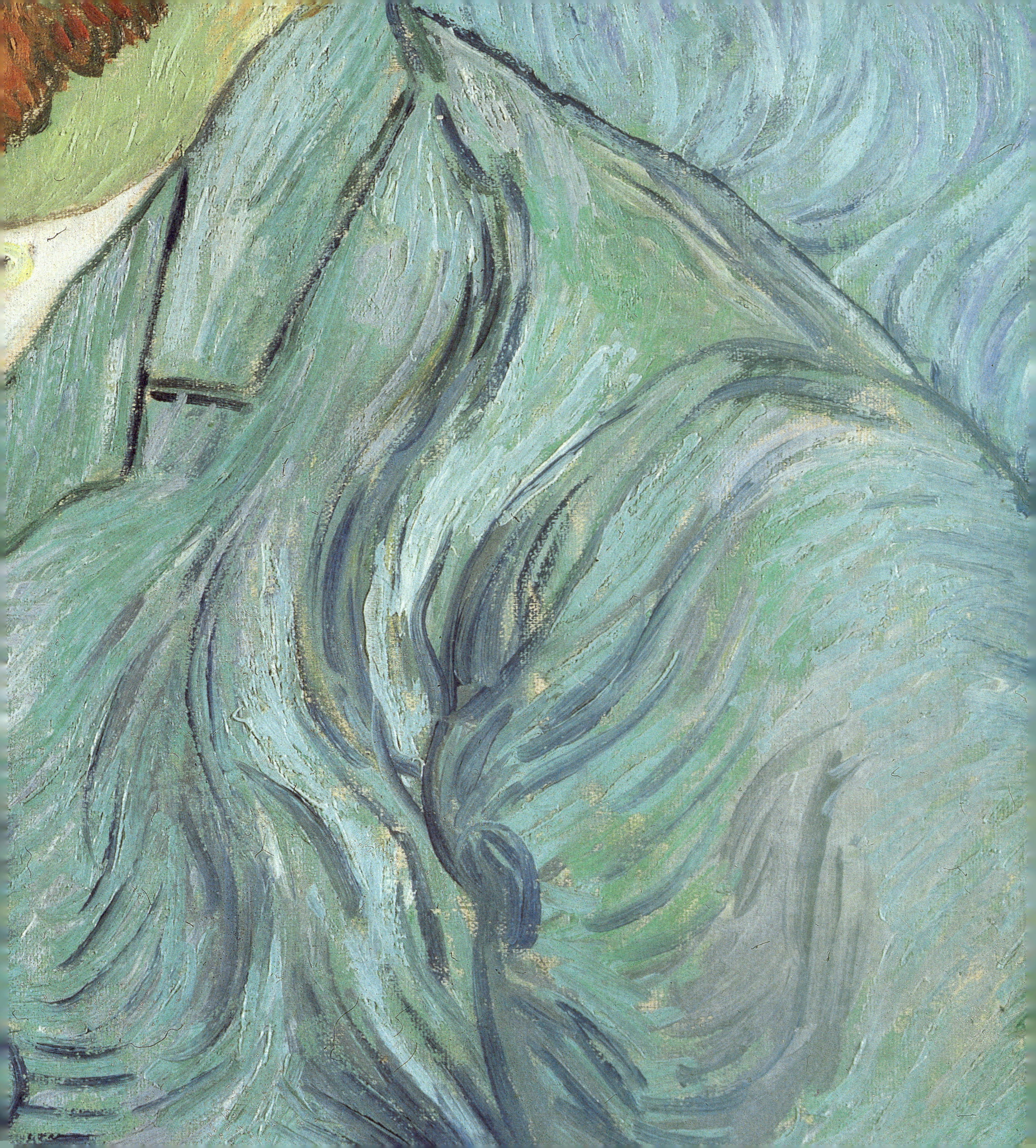

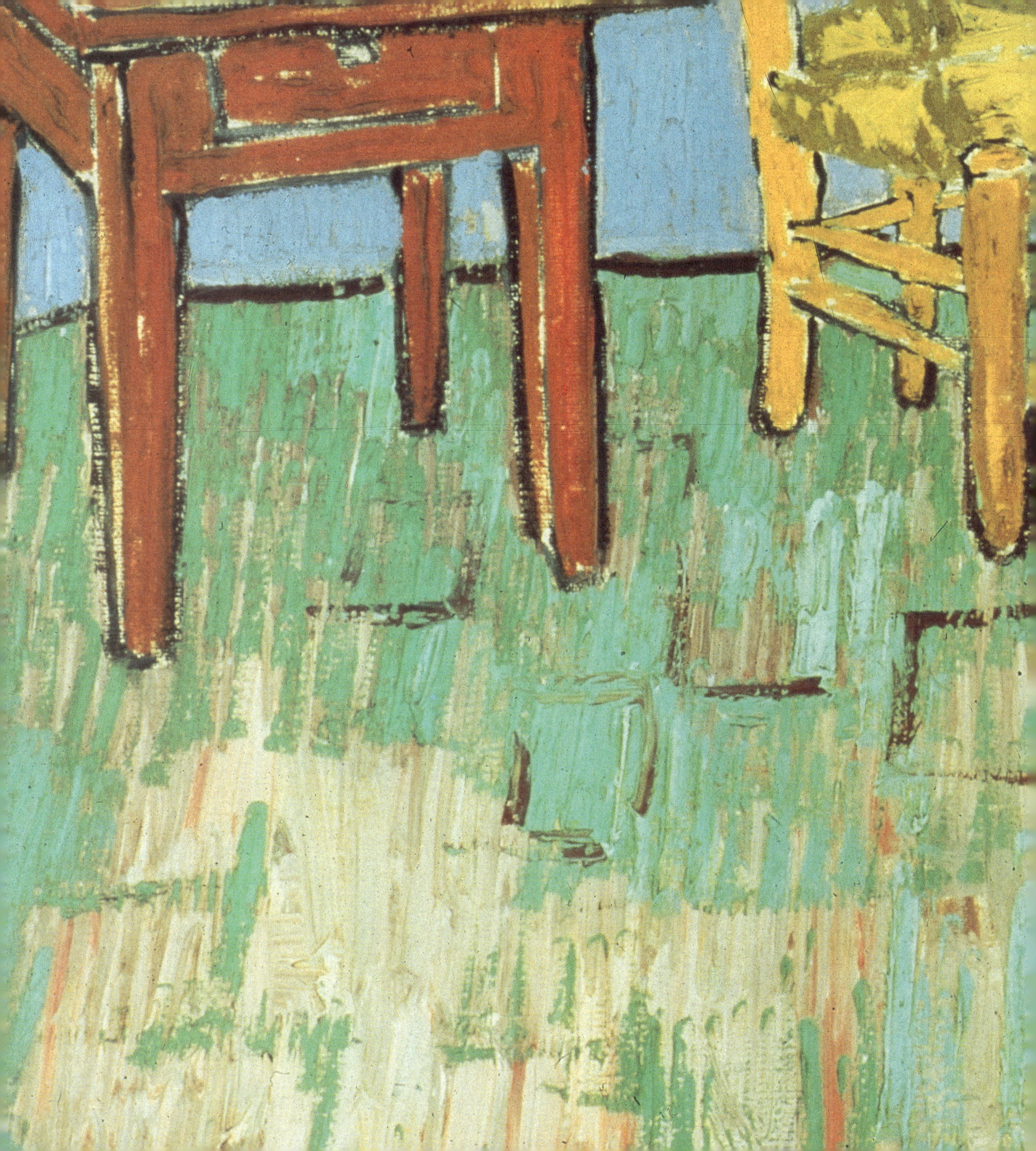

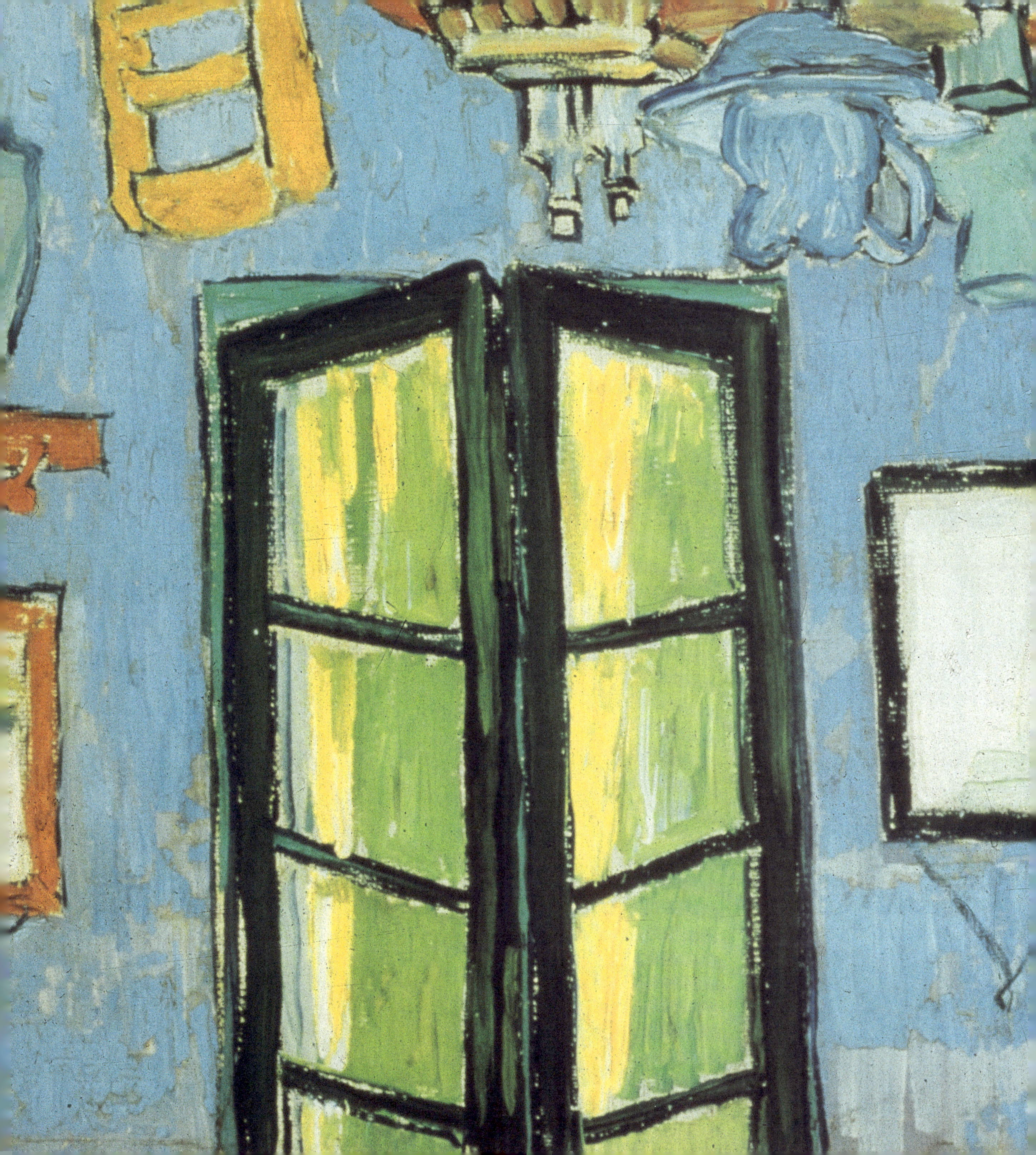

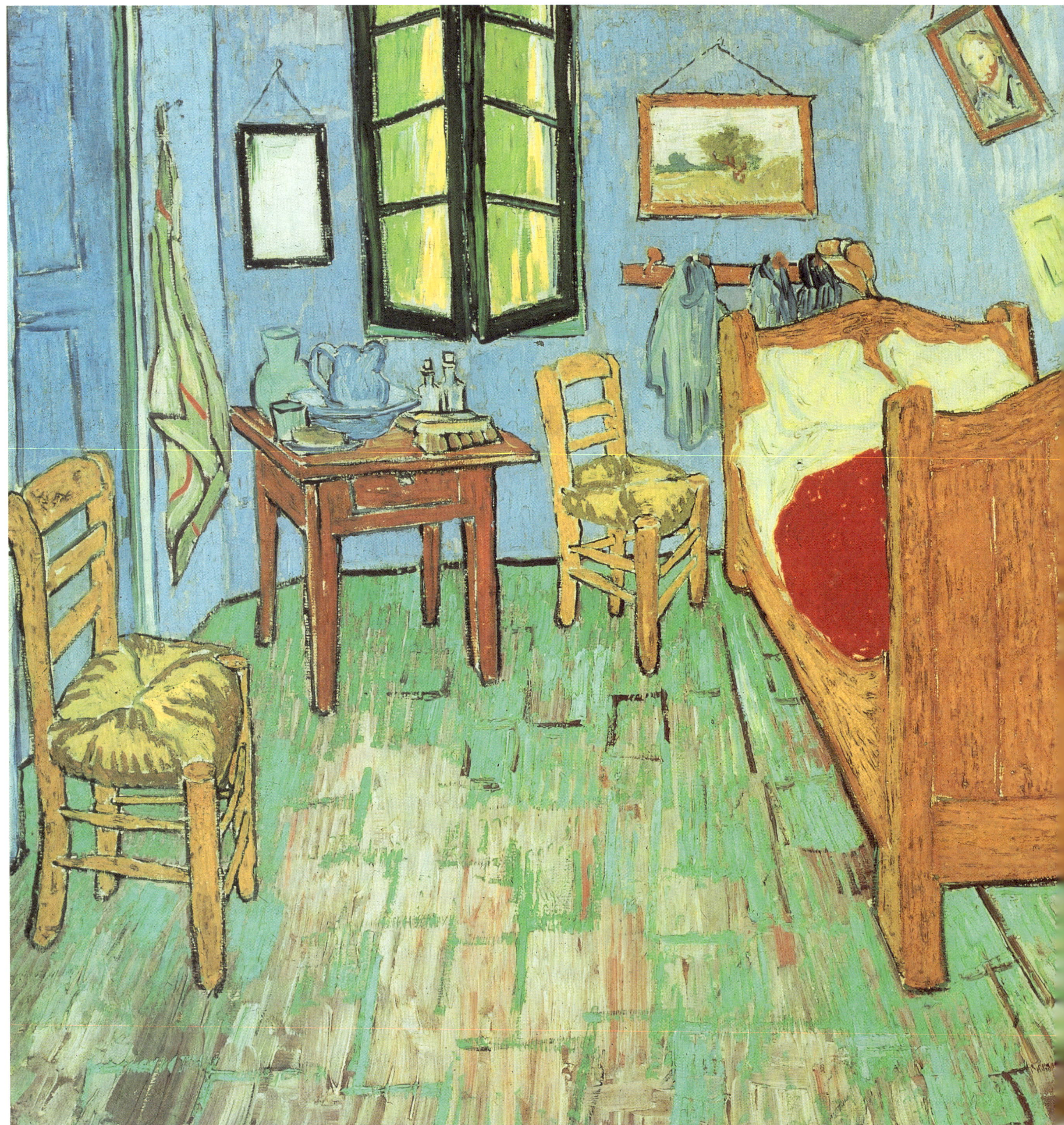

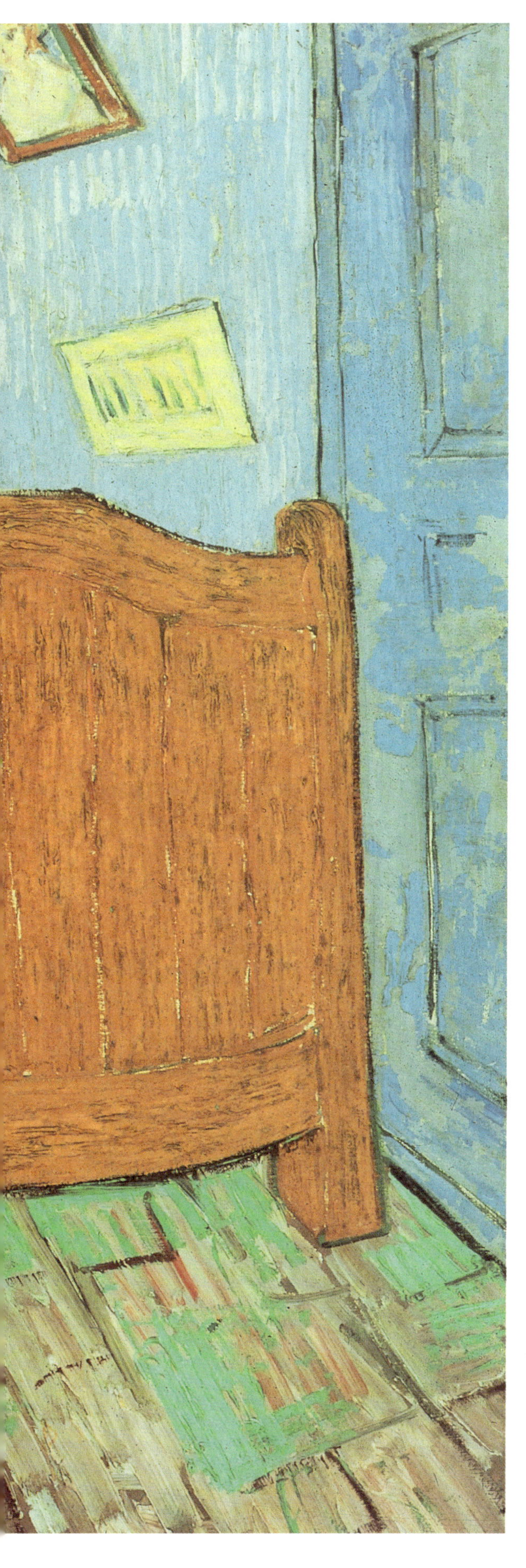

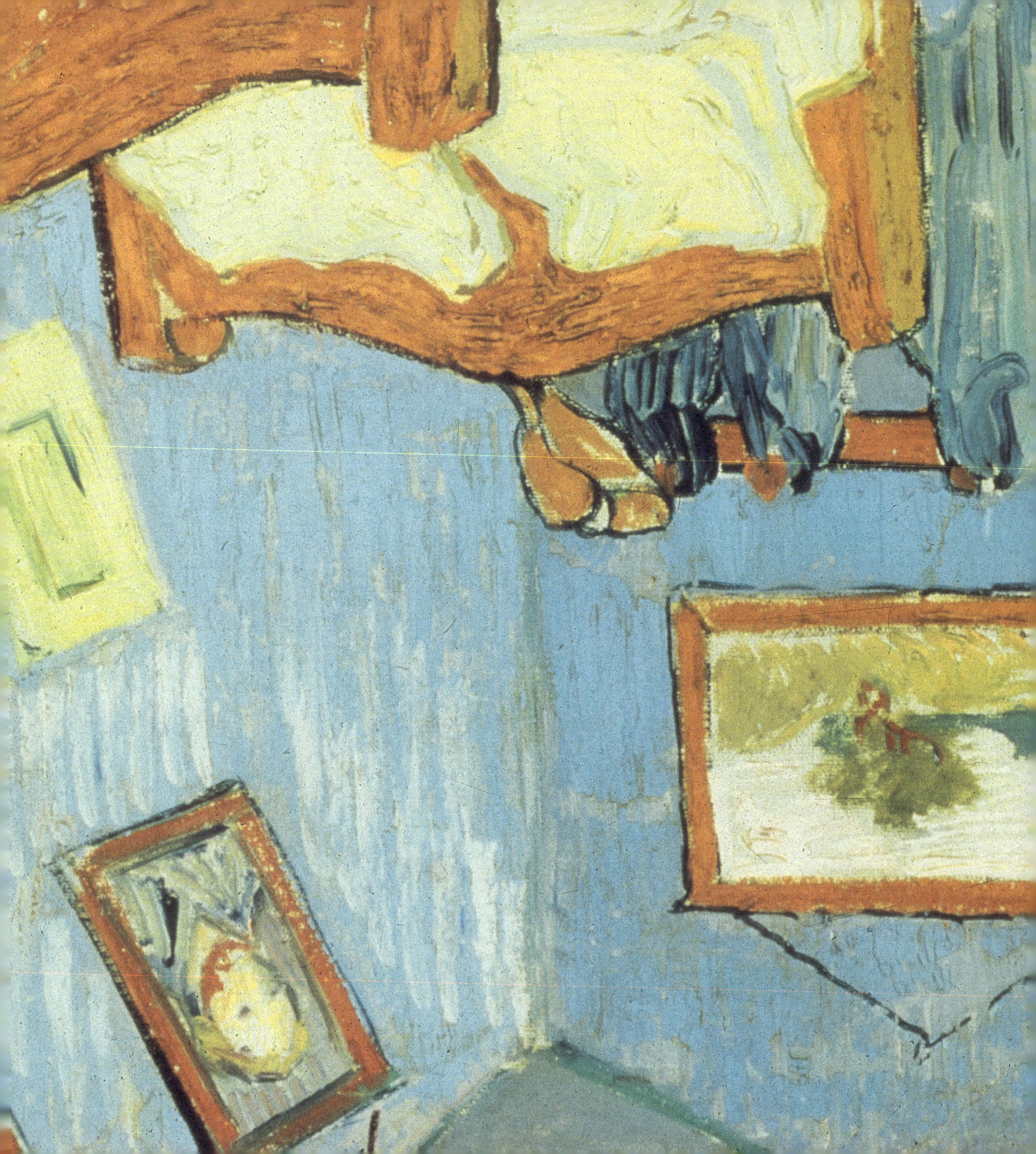

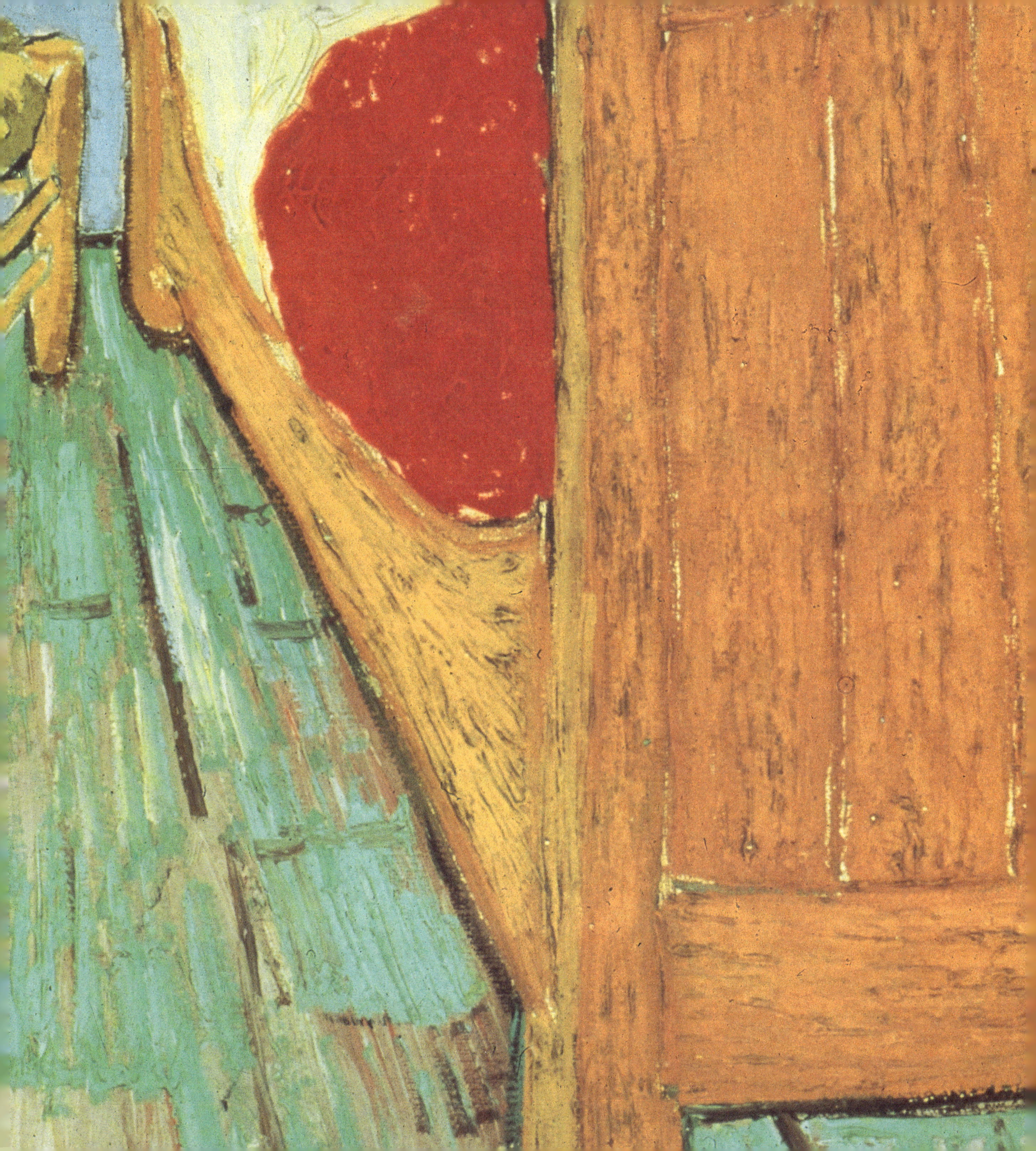

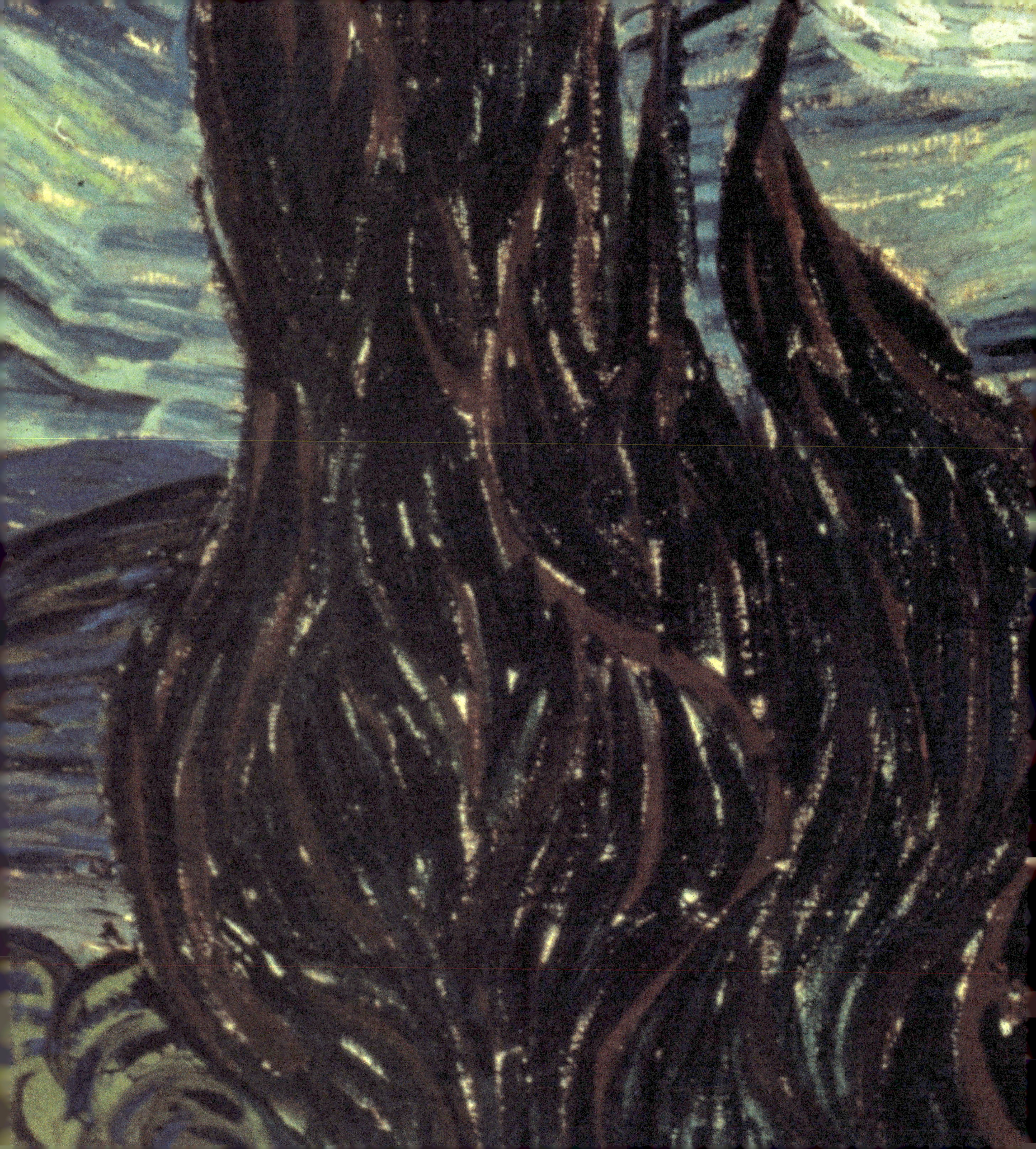

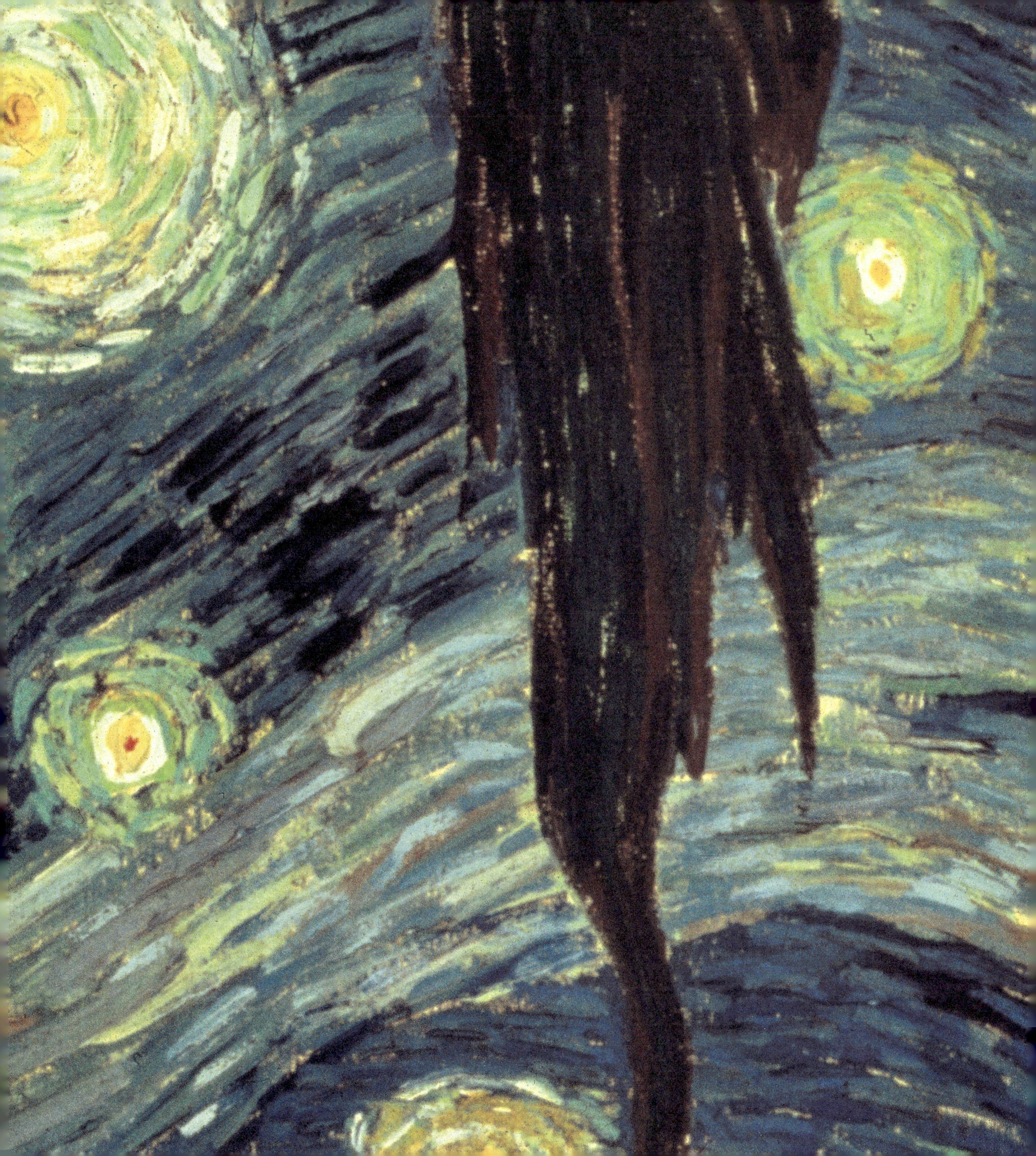

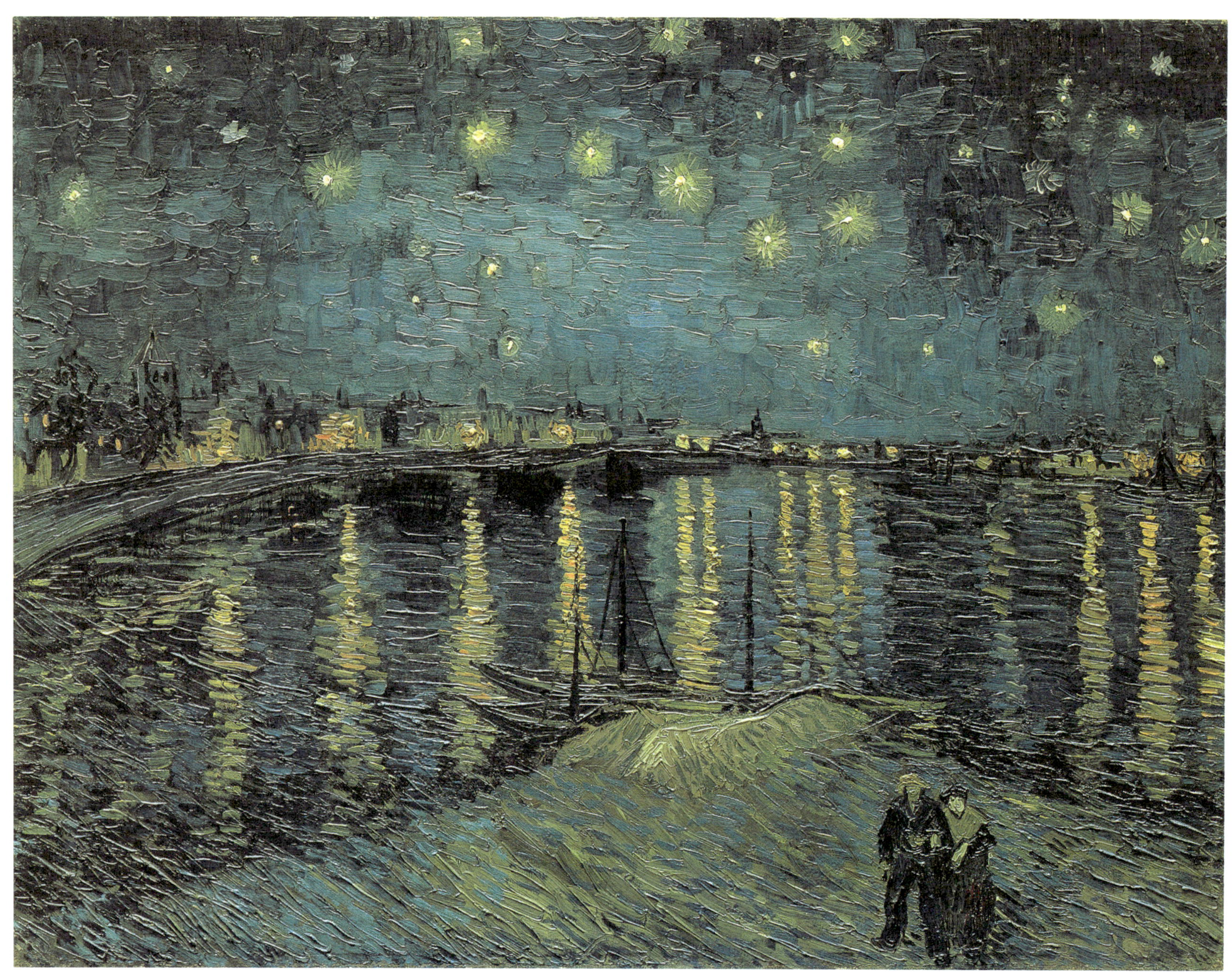

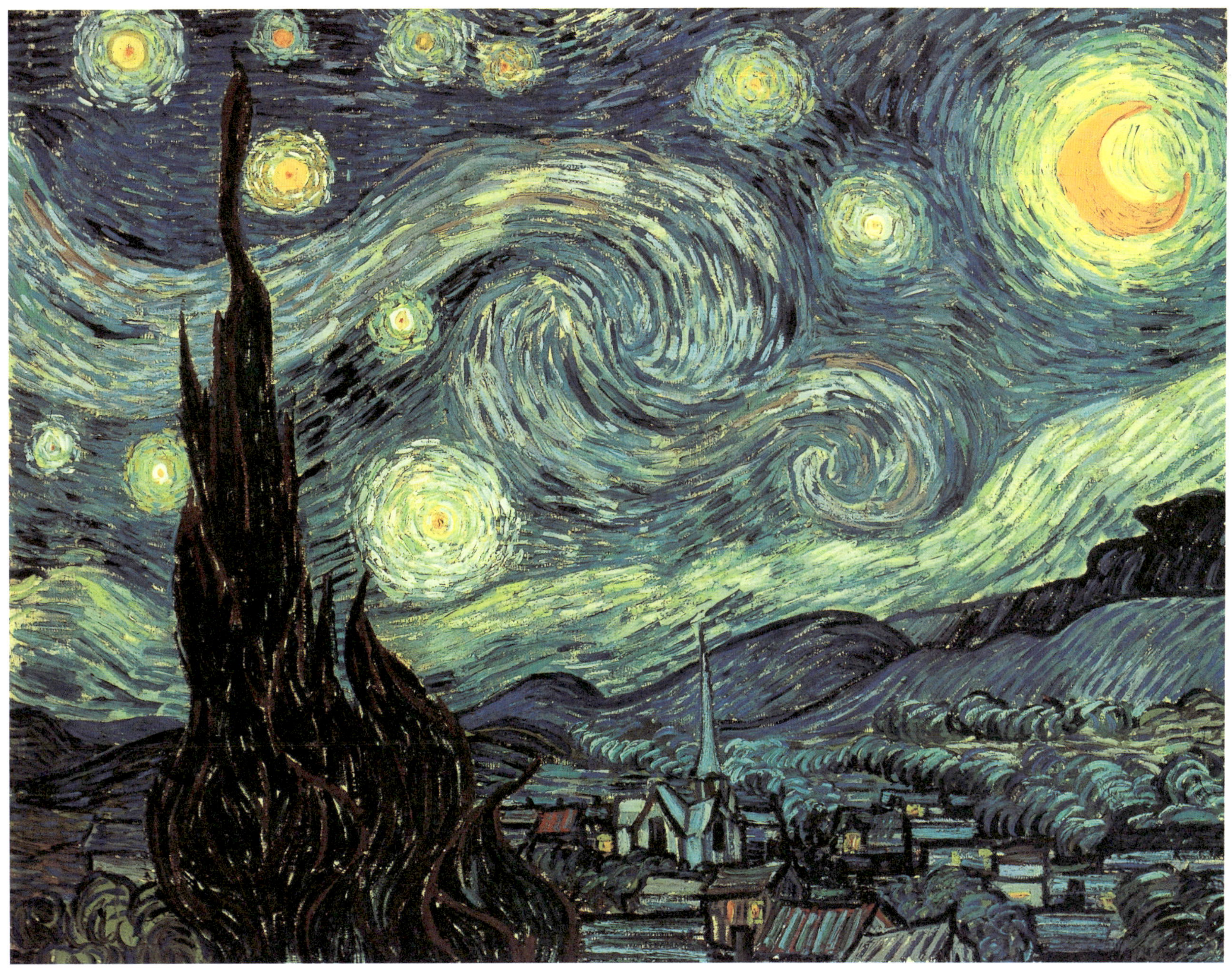

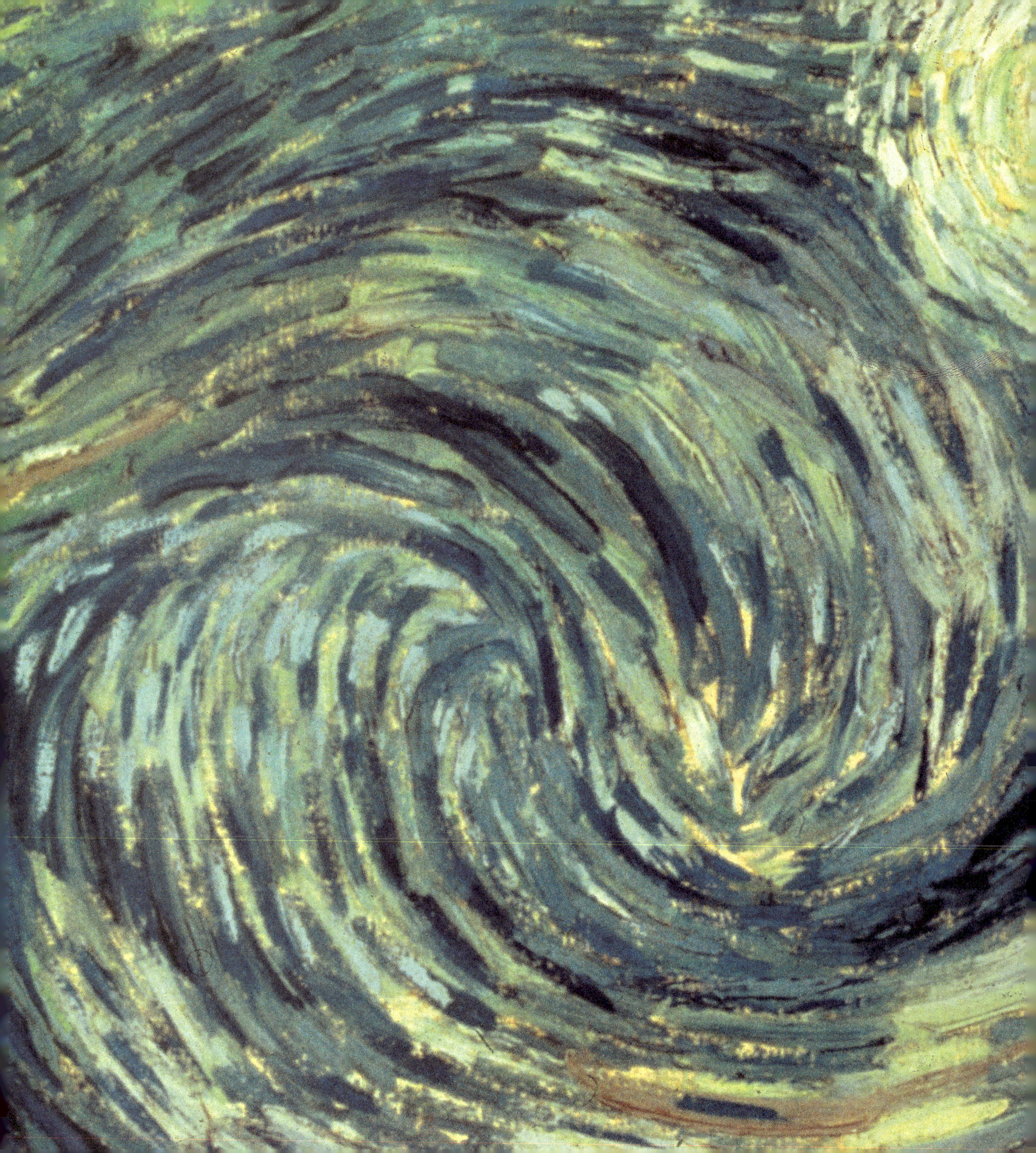

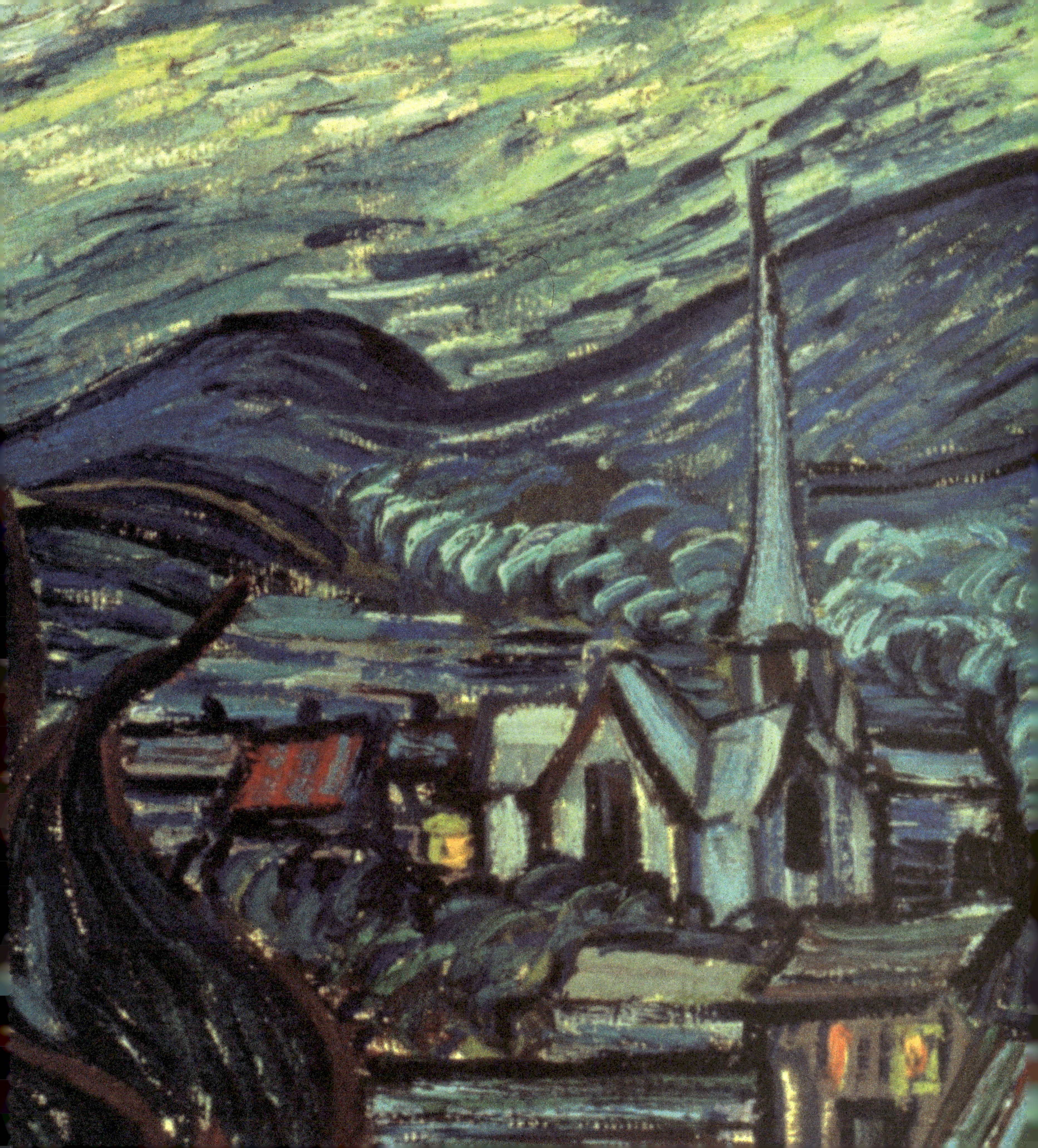

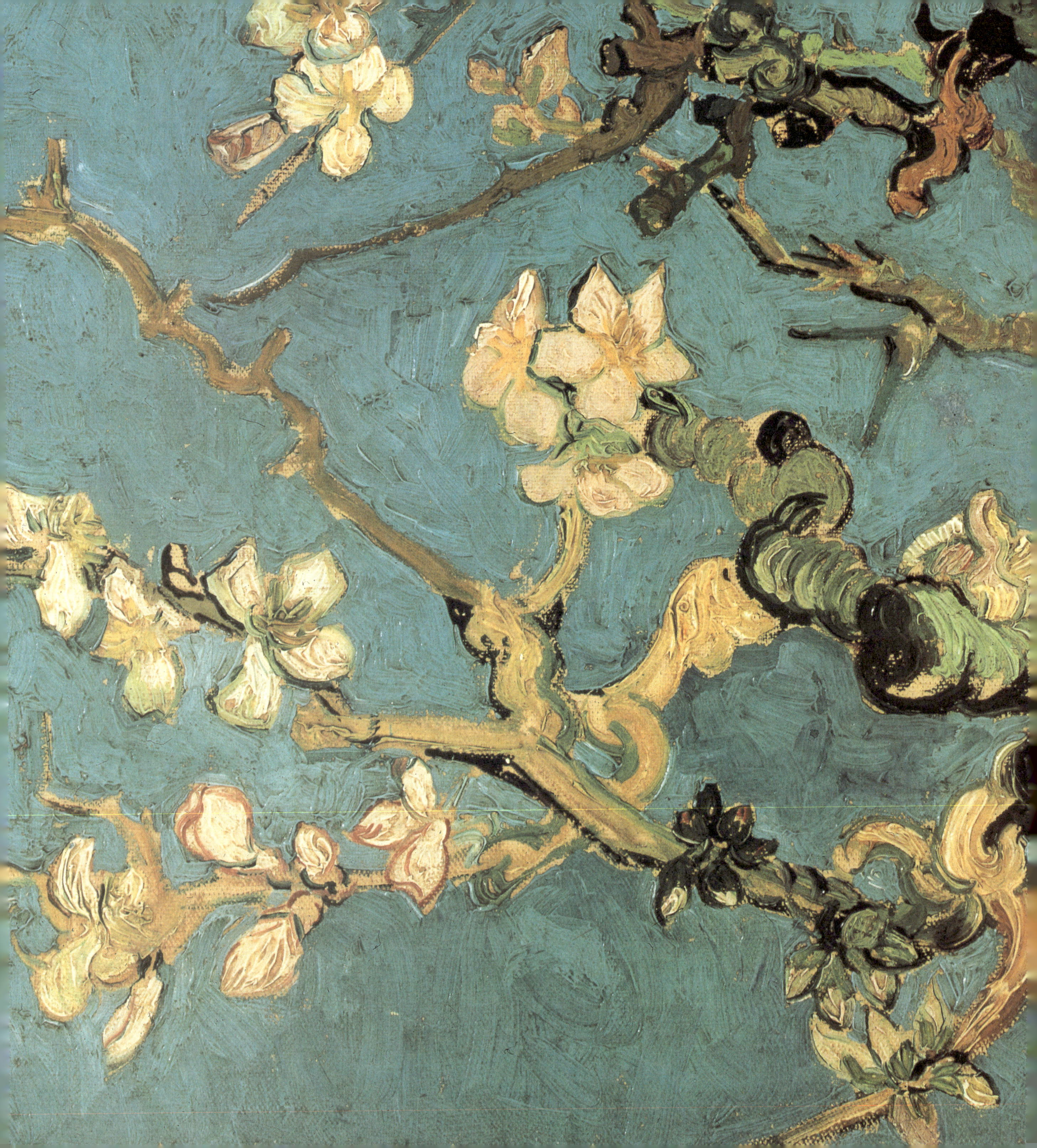

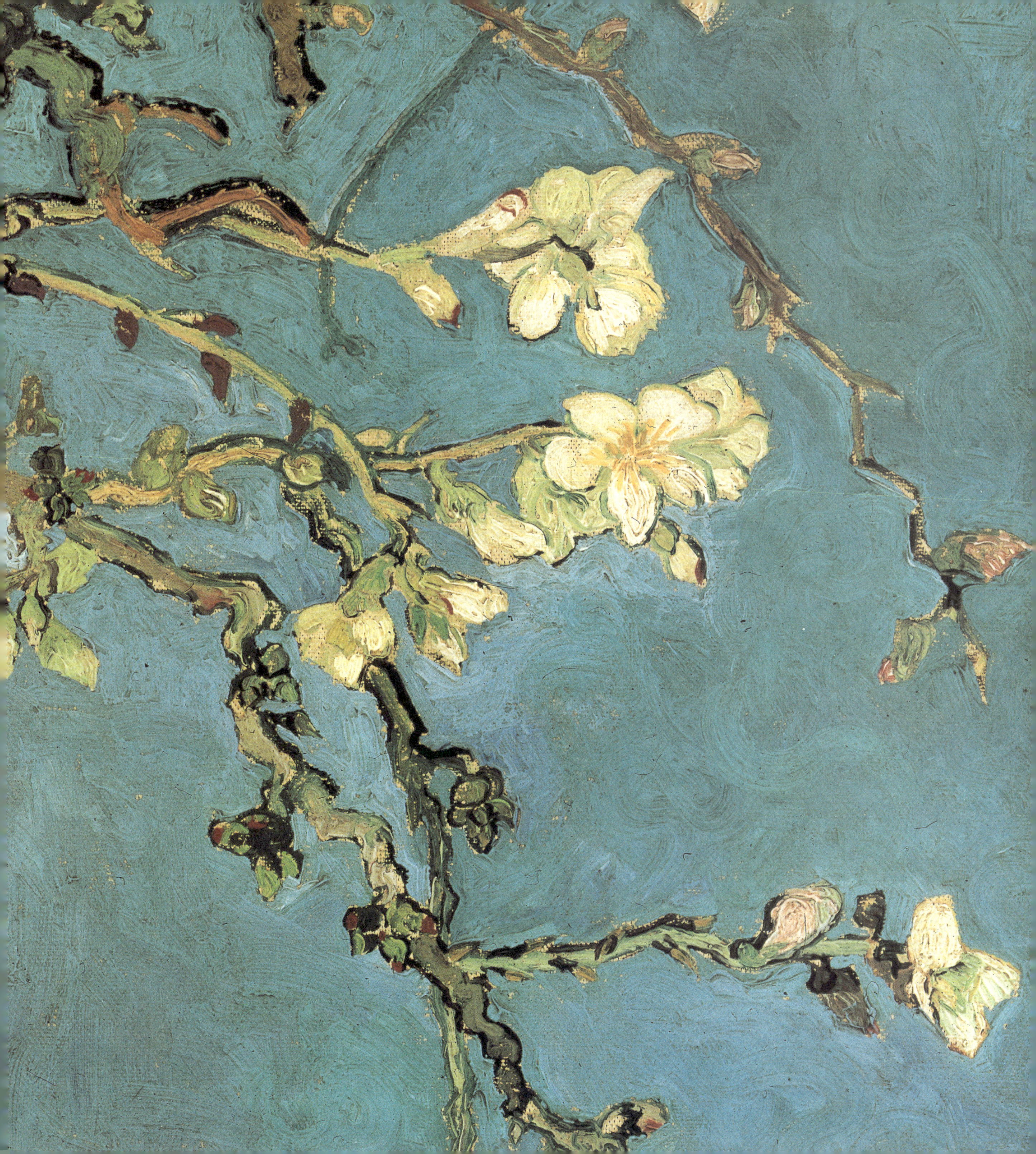

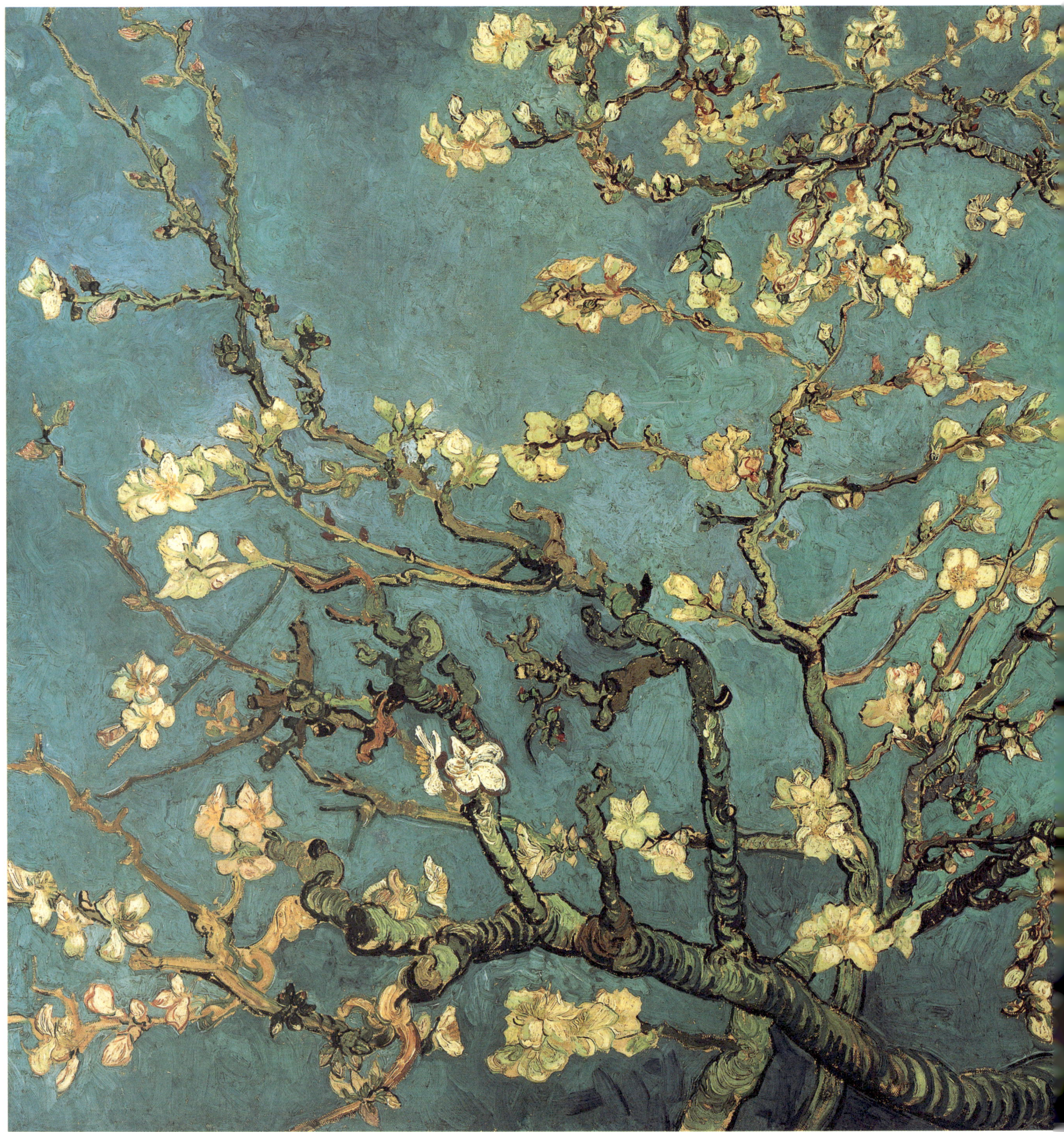

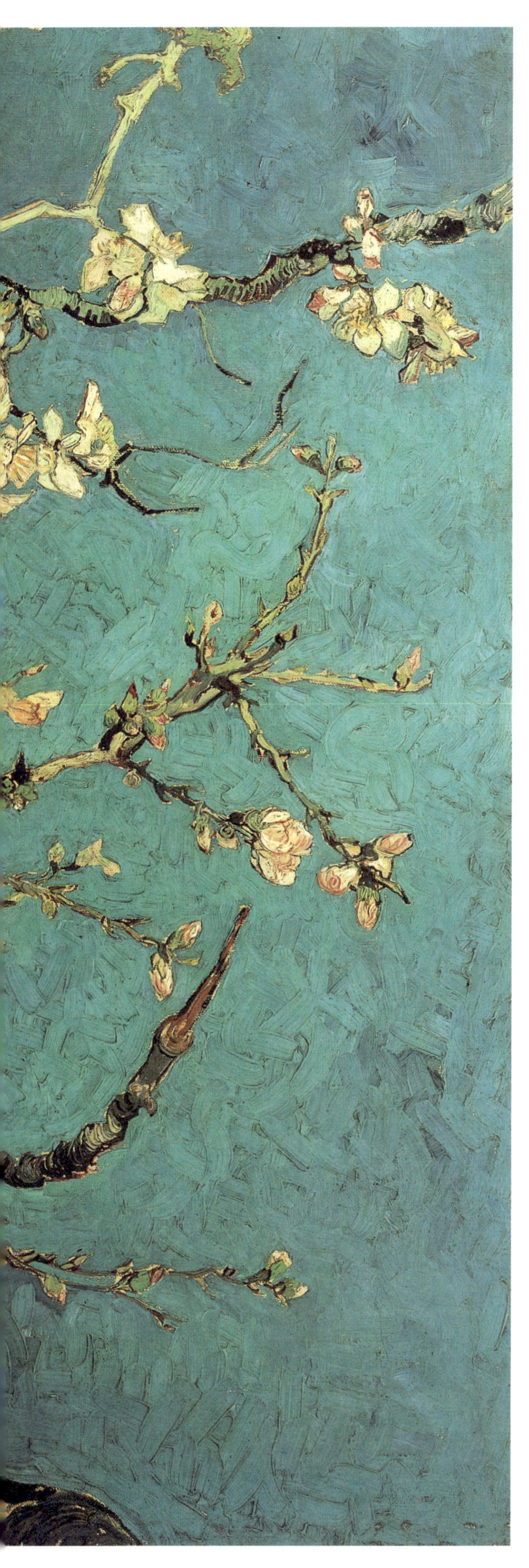

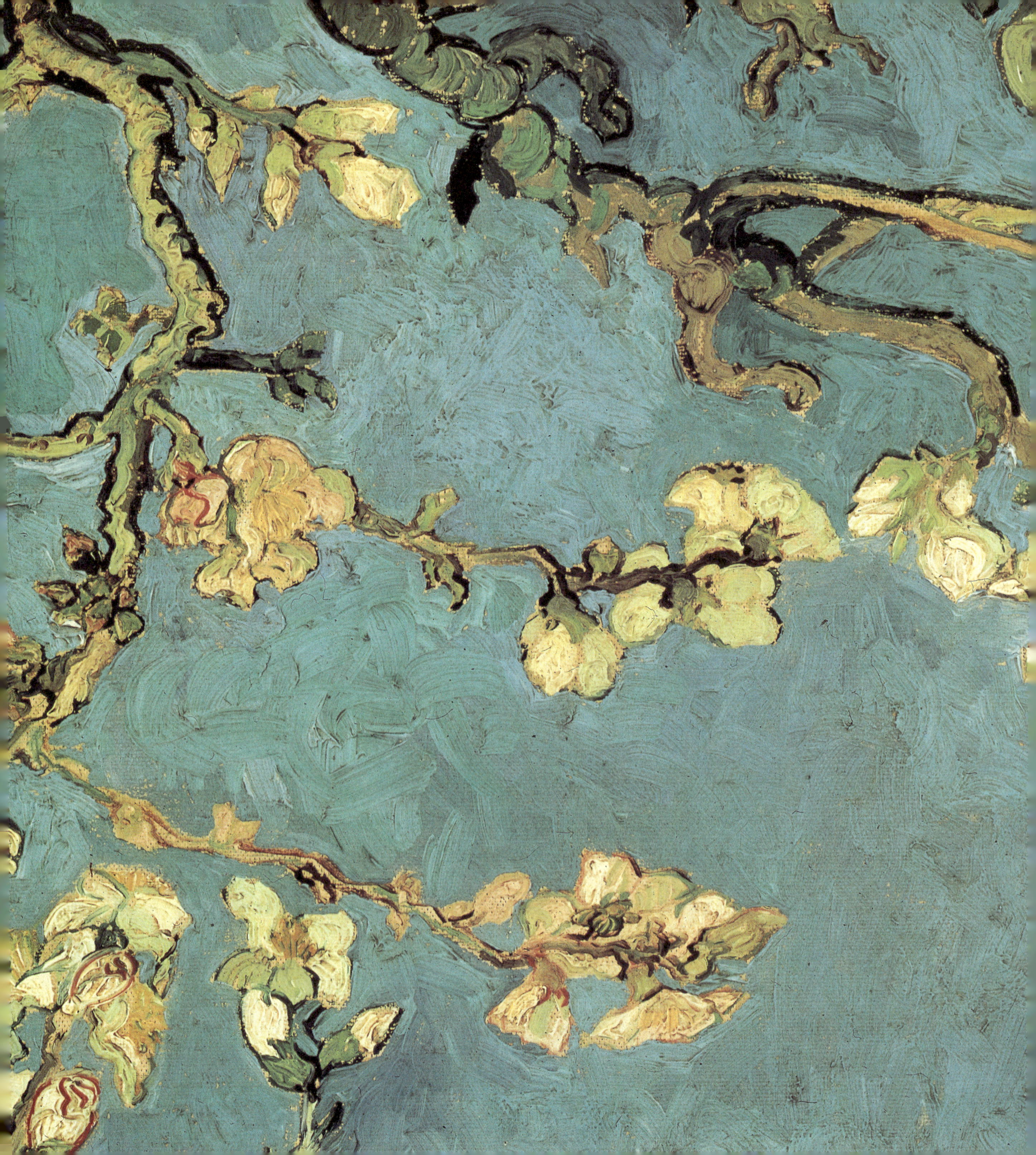

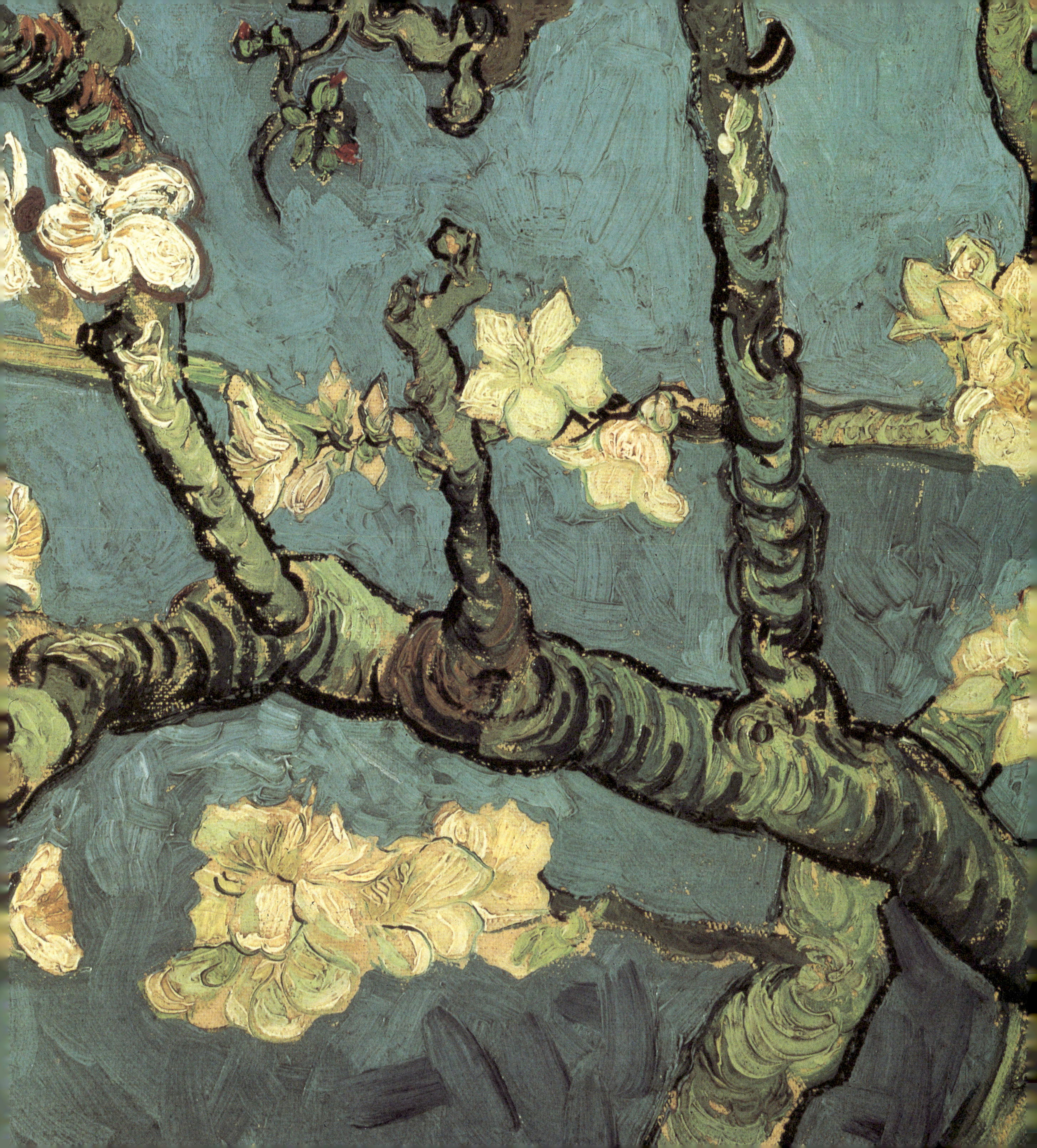

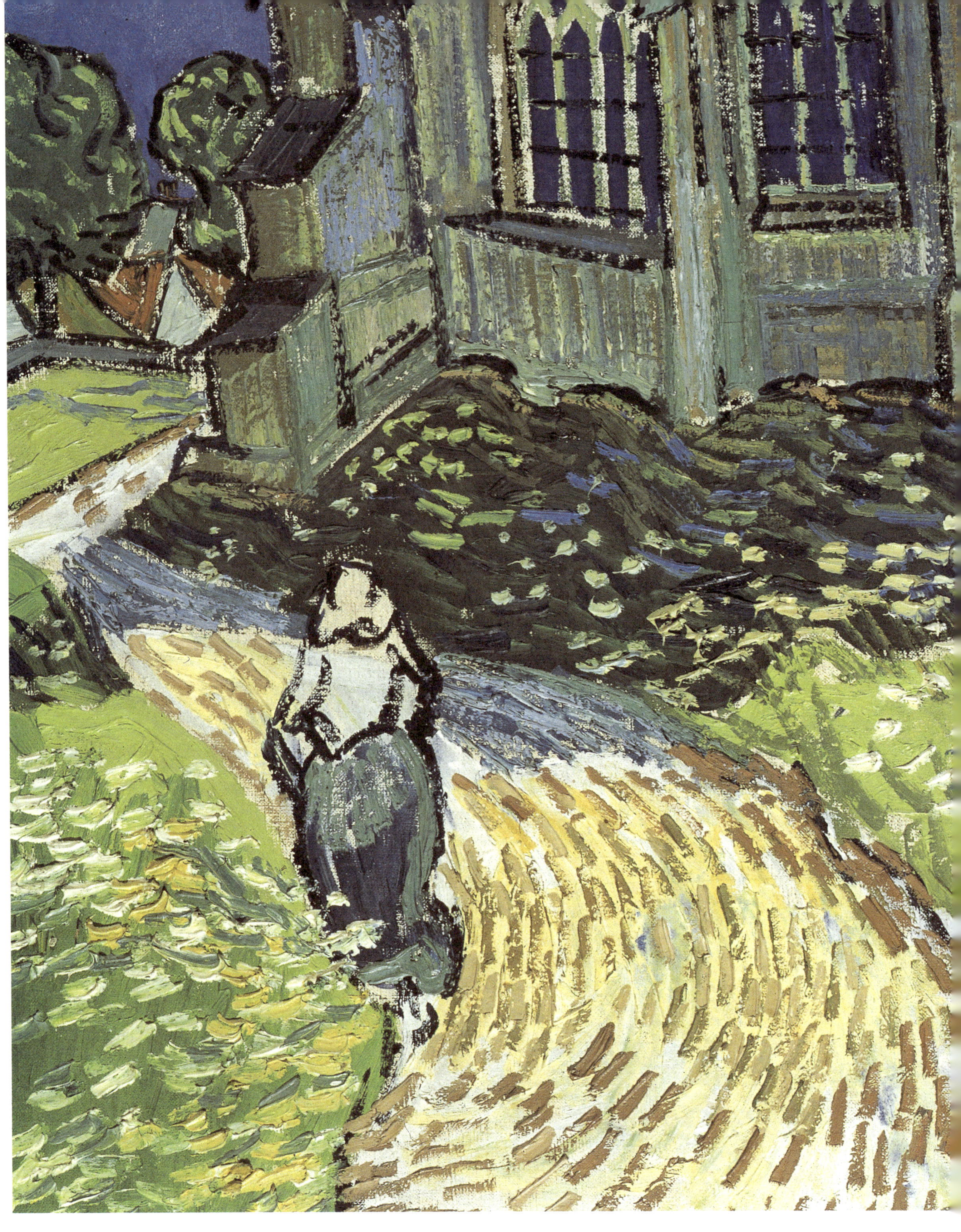

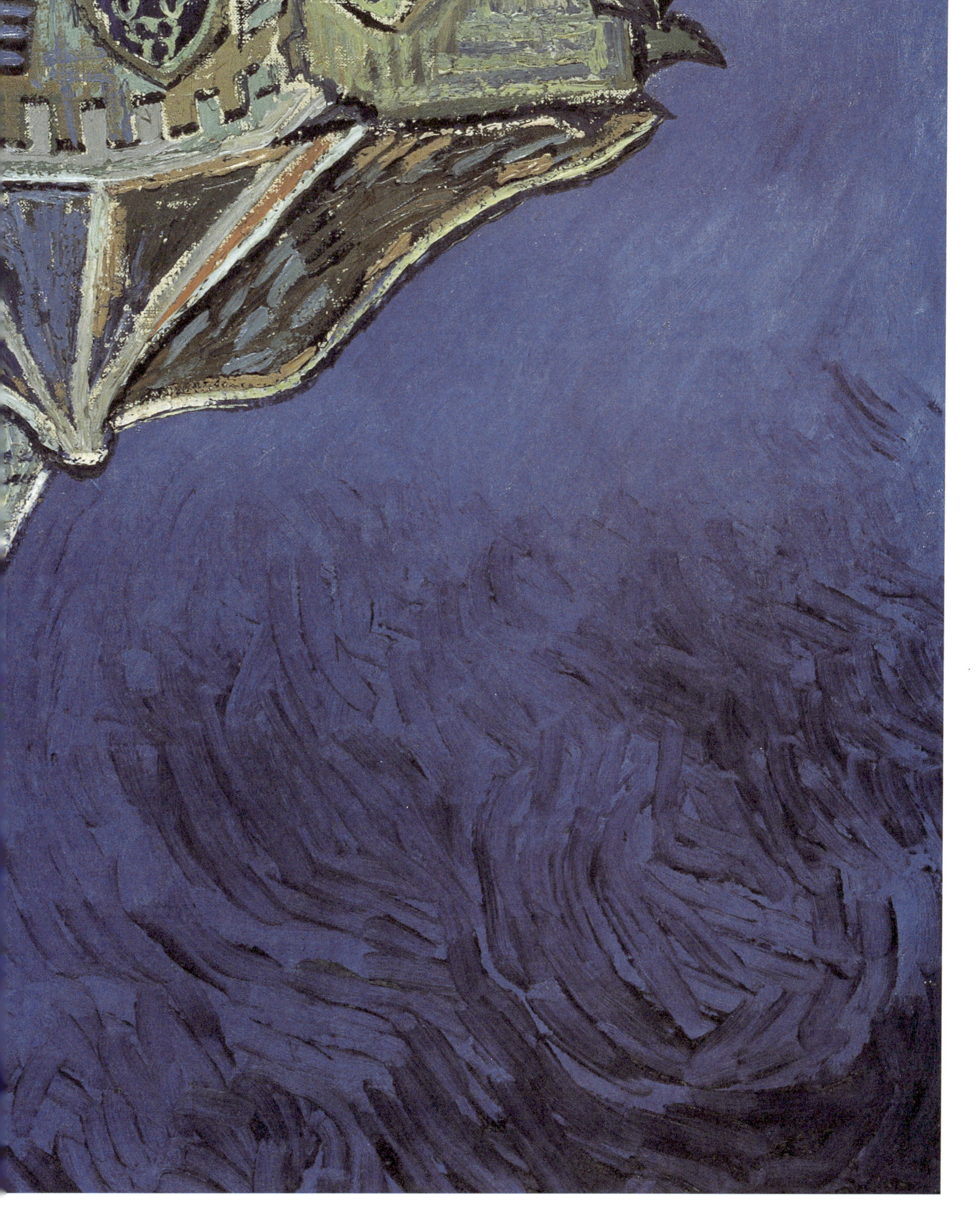

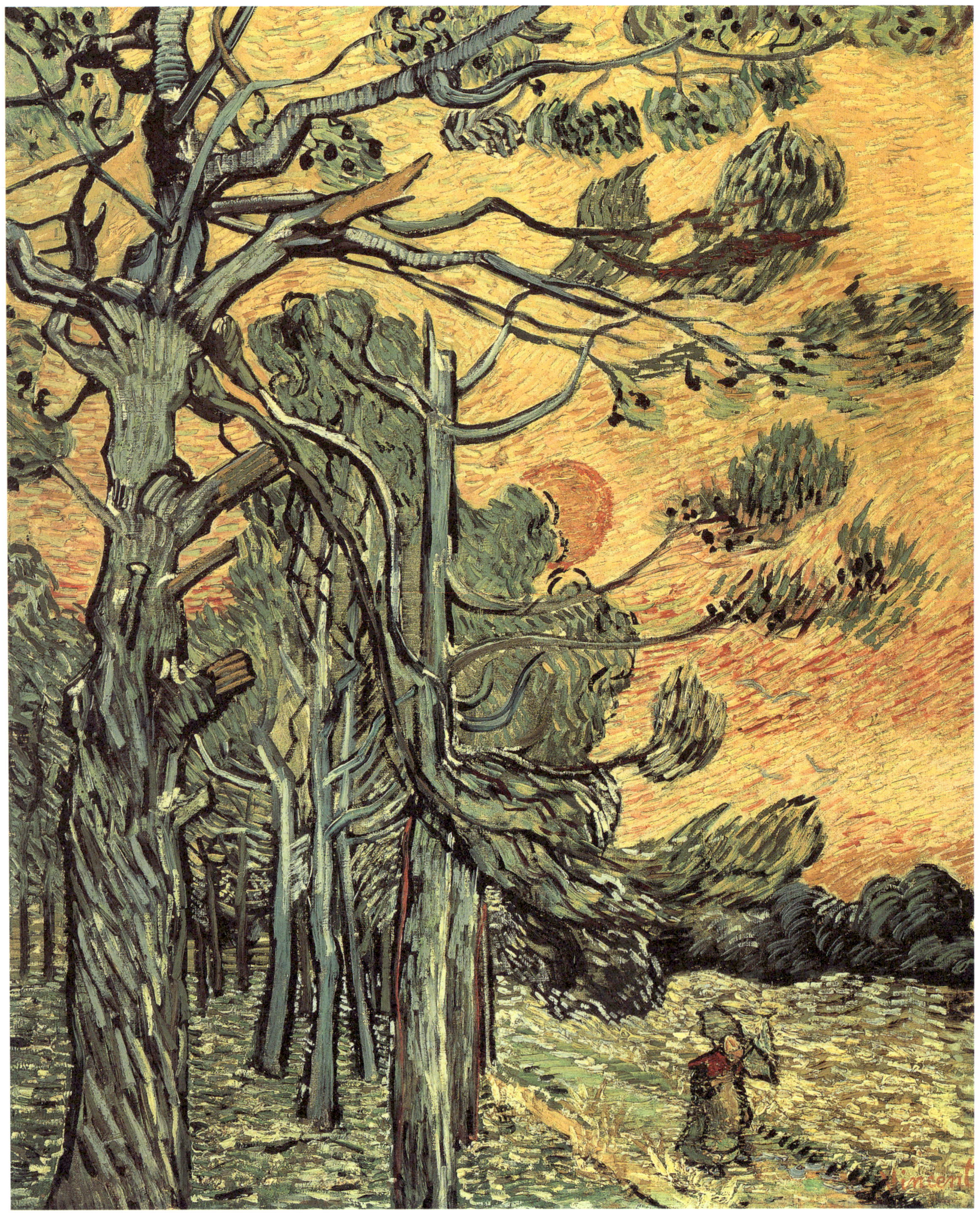
Vincent

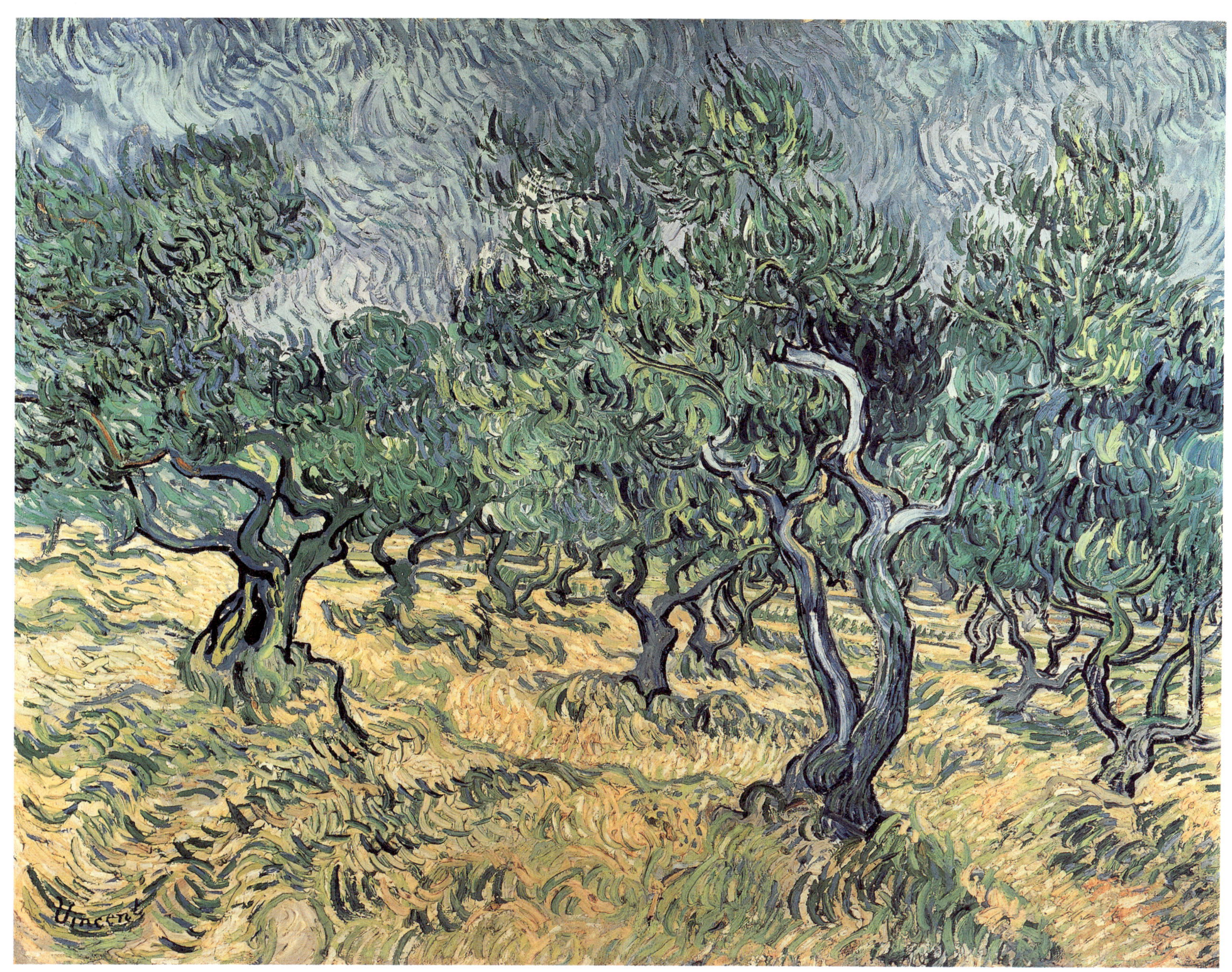
Vincent

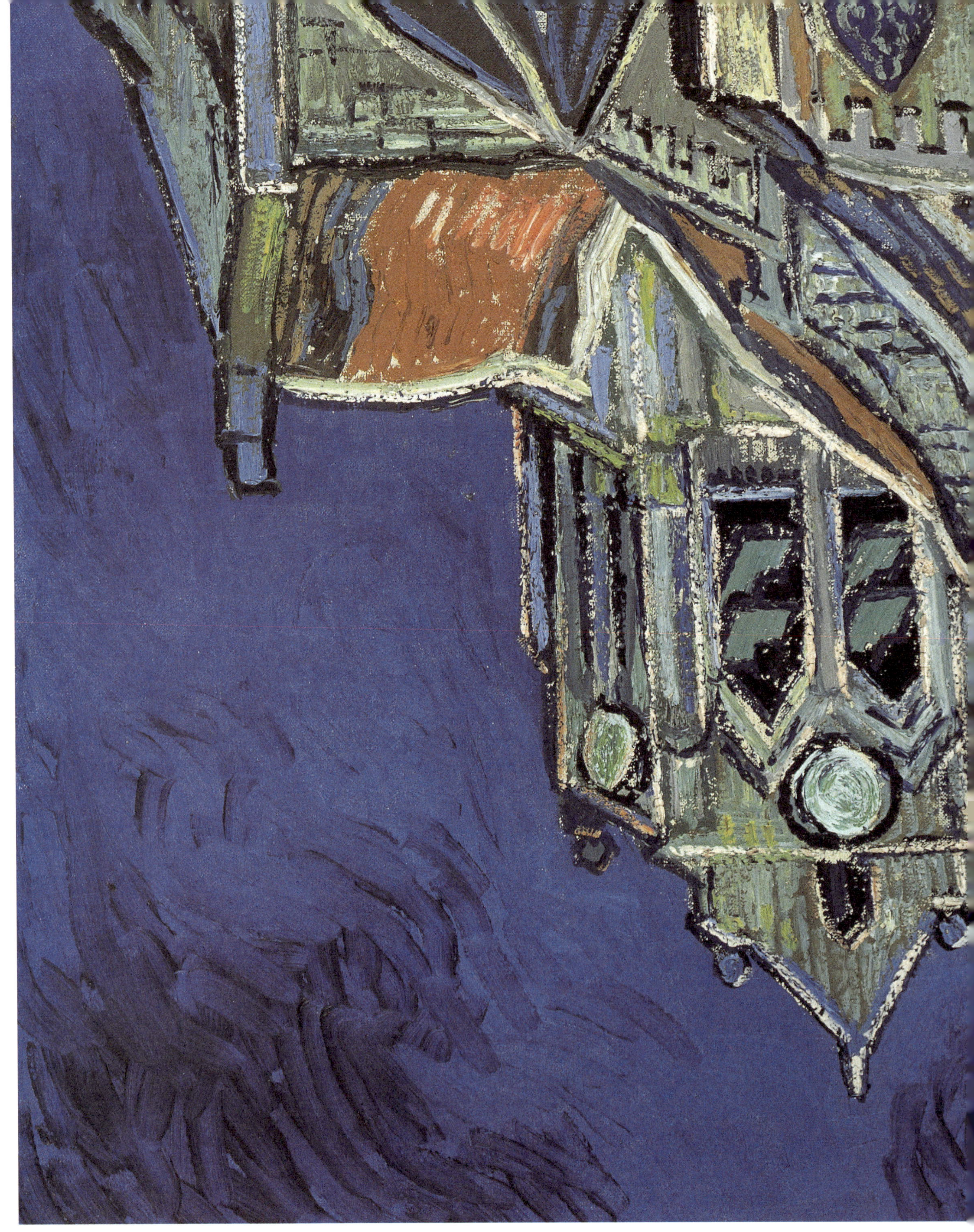

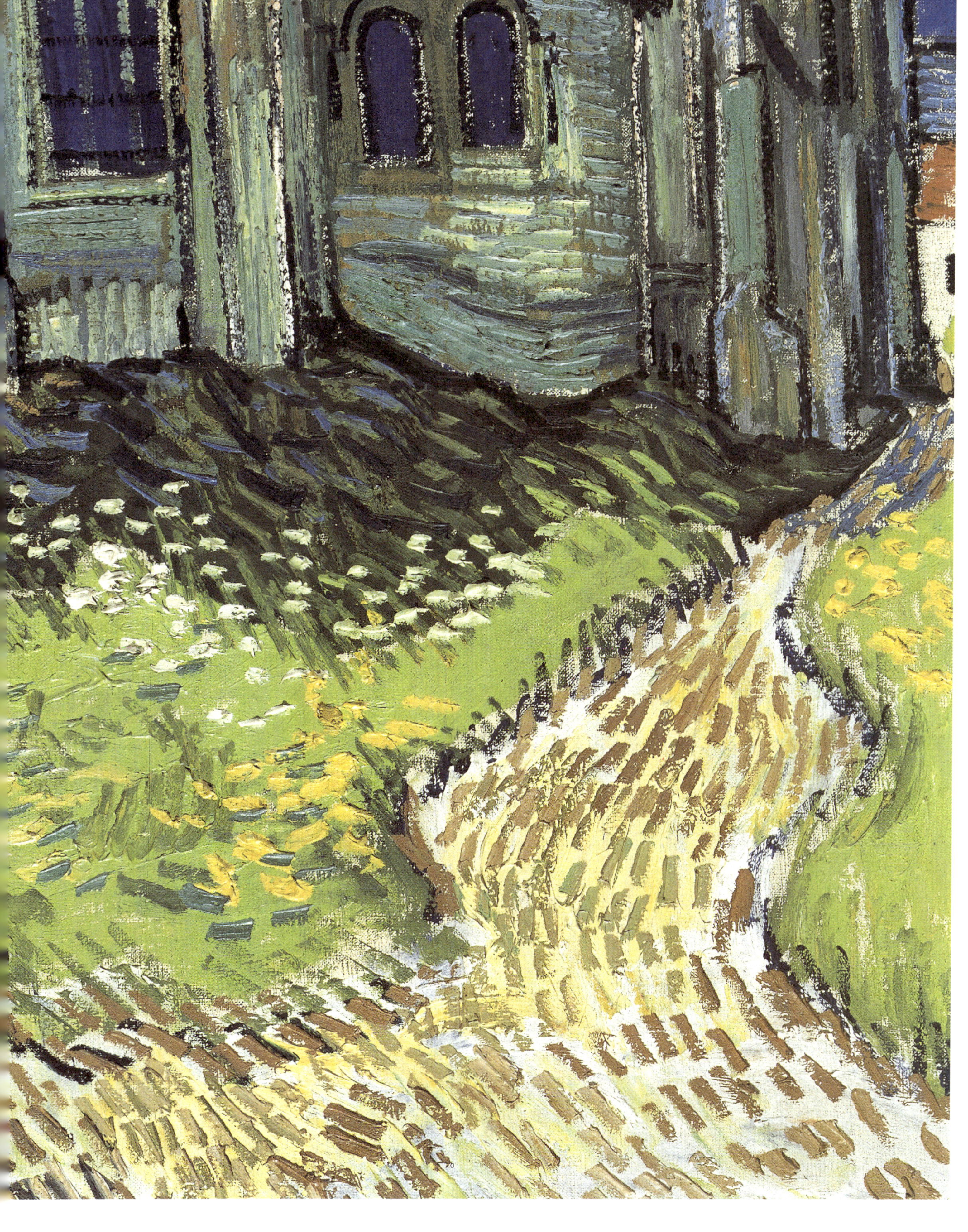

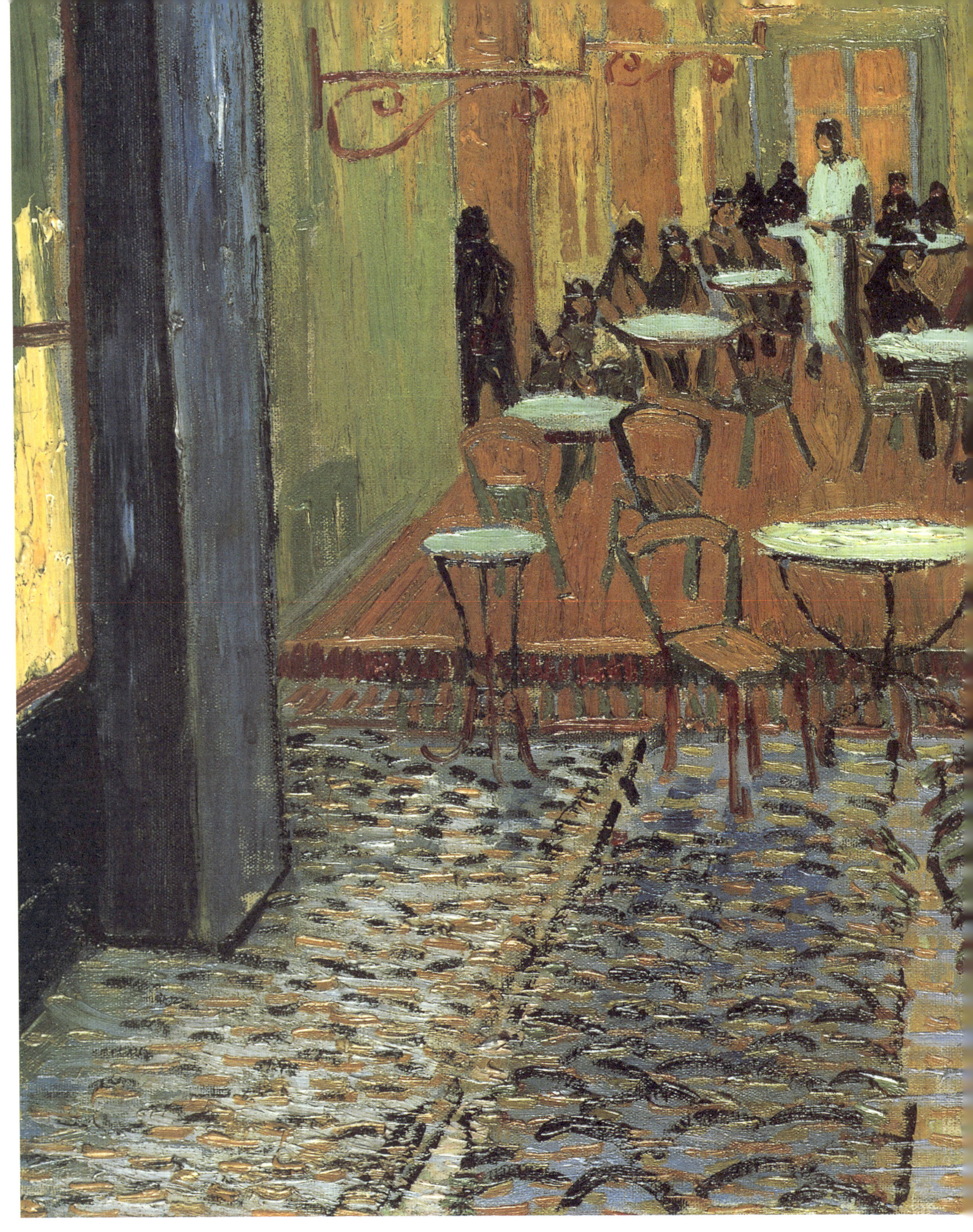

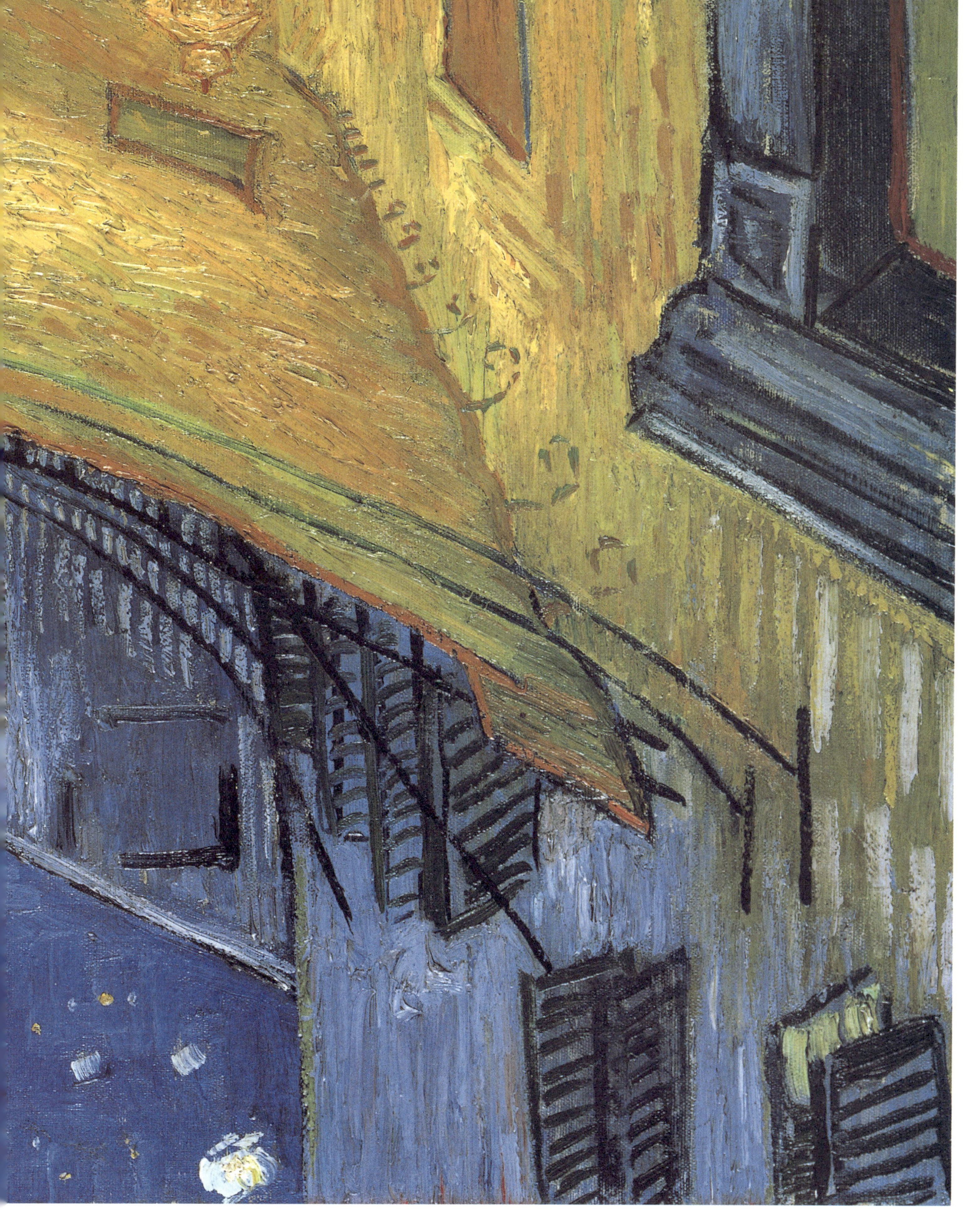

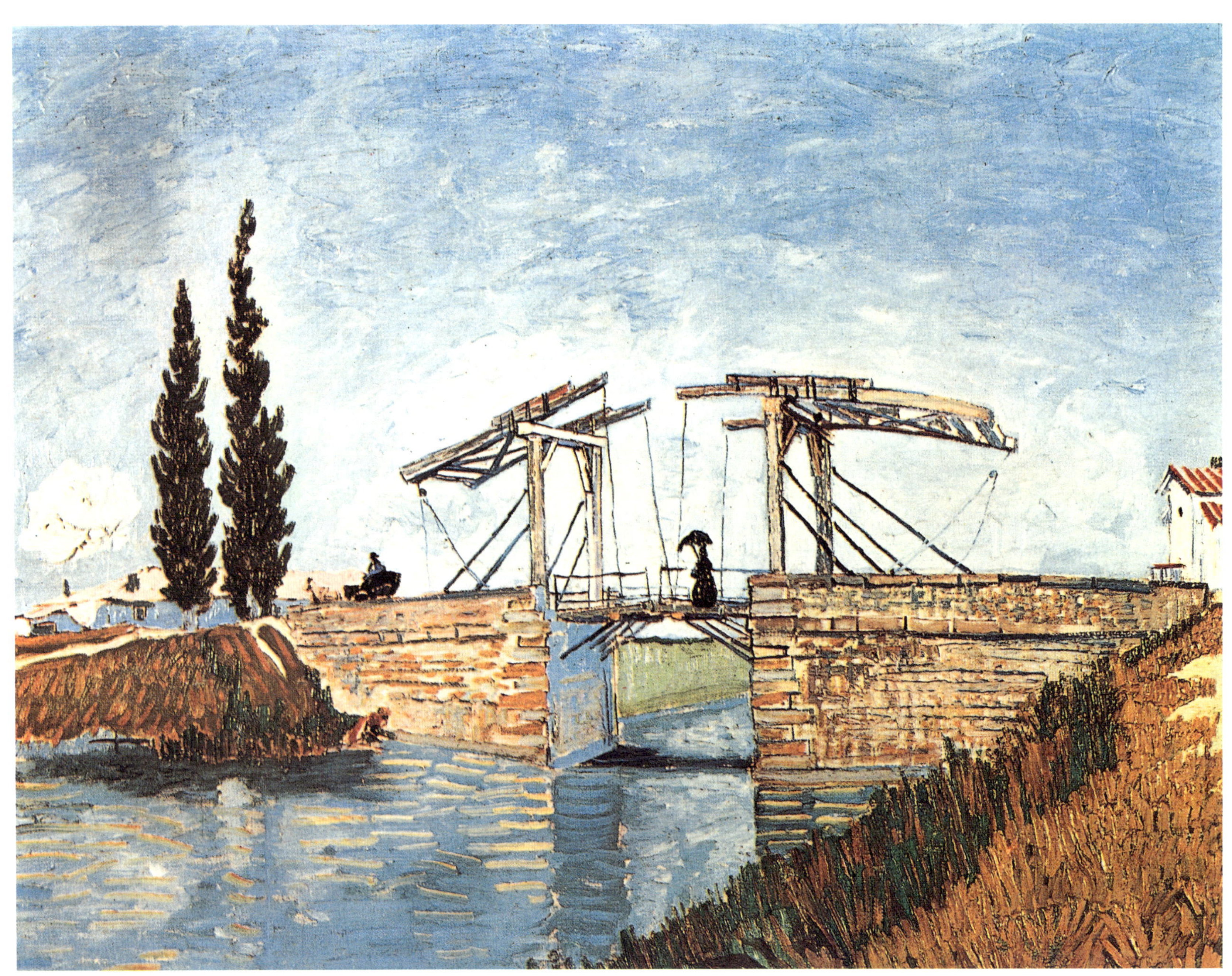

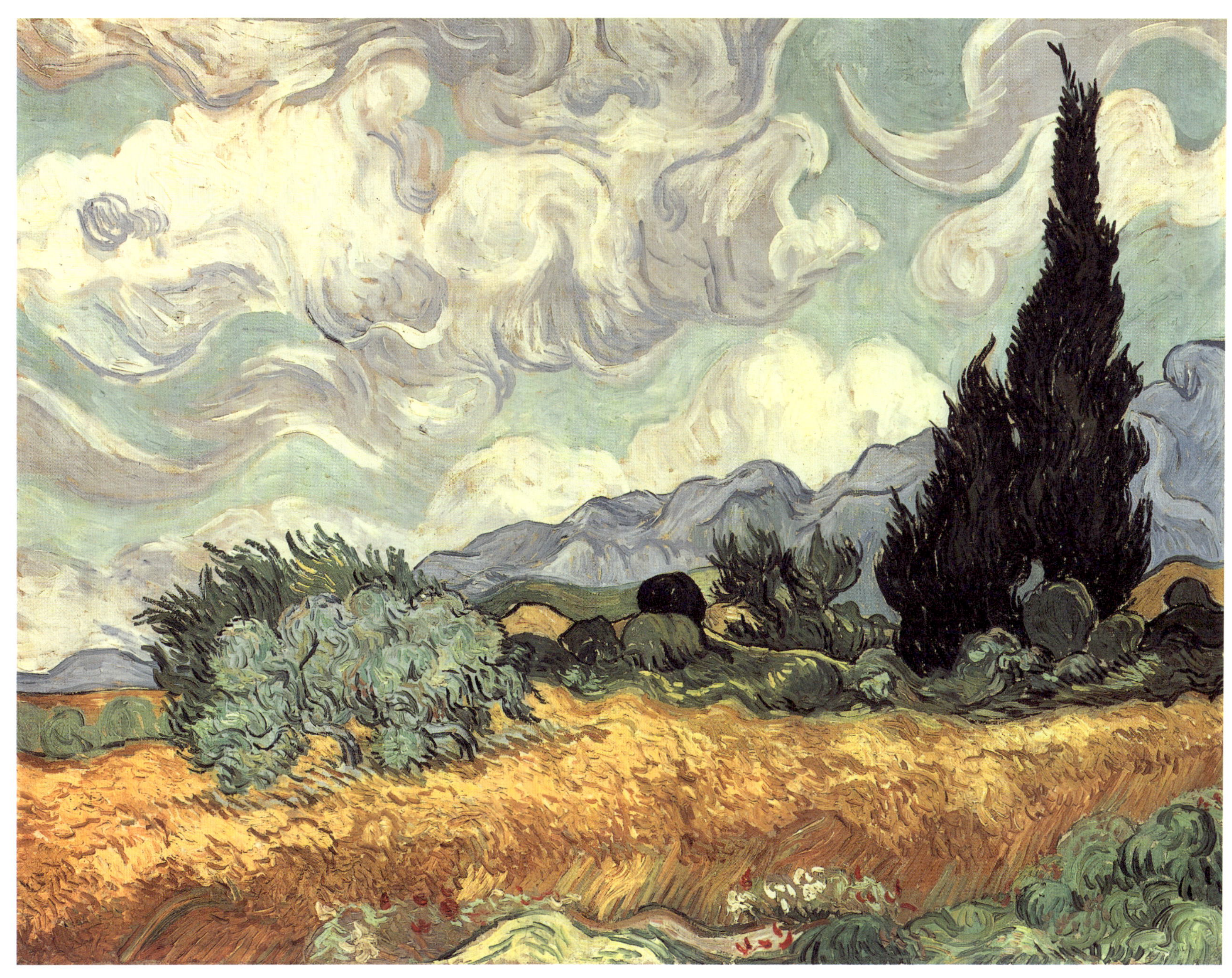

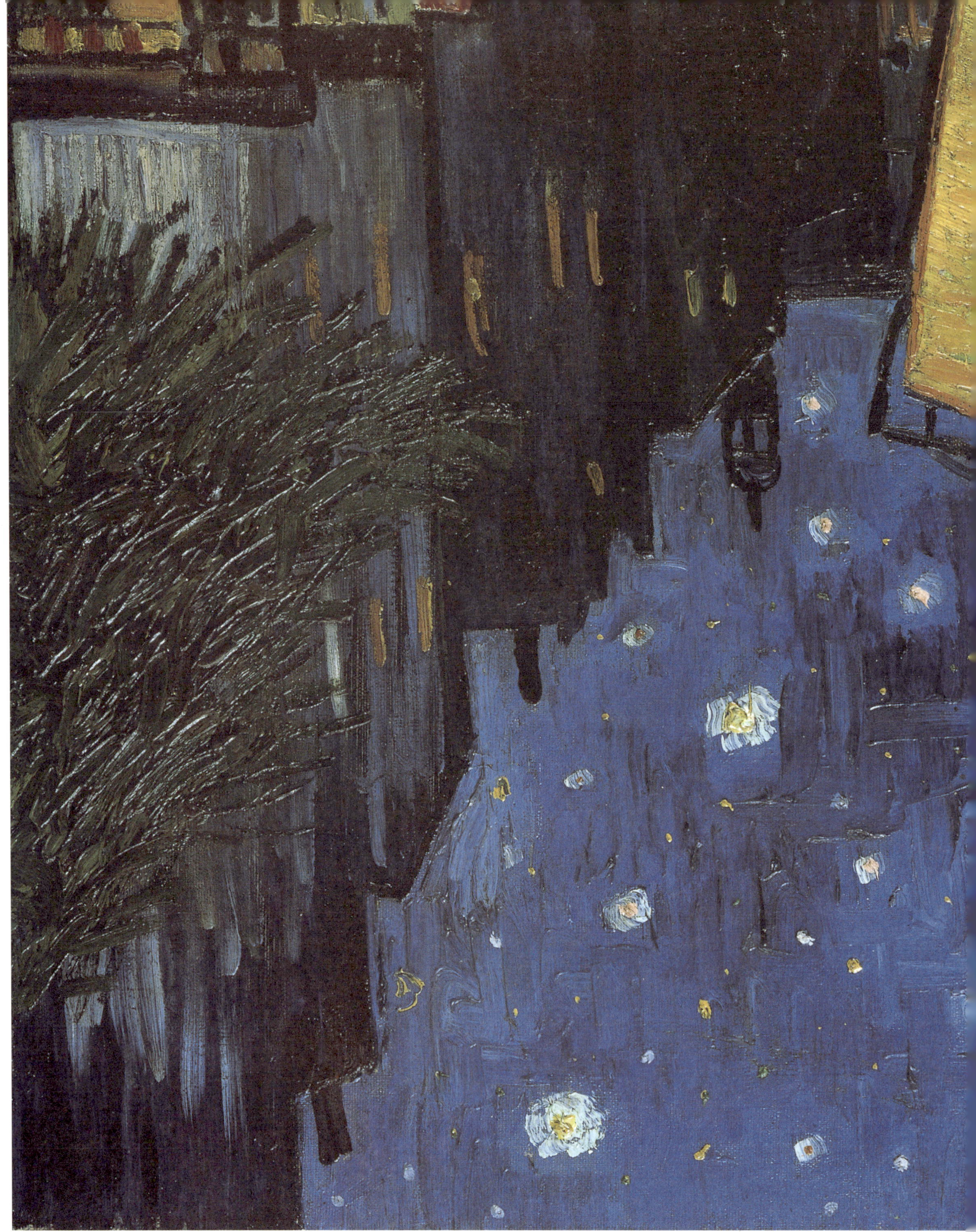

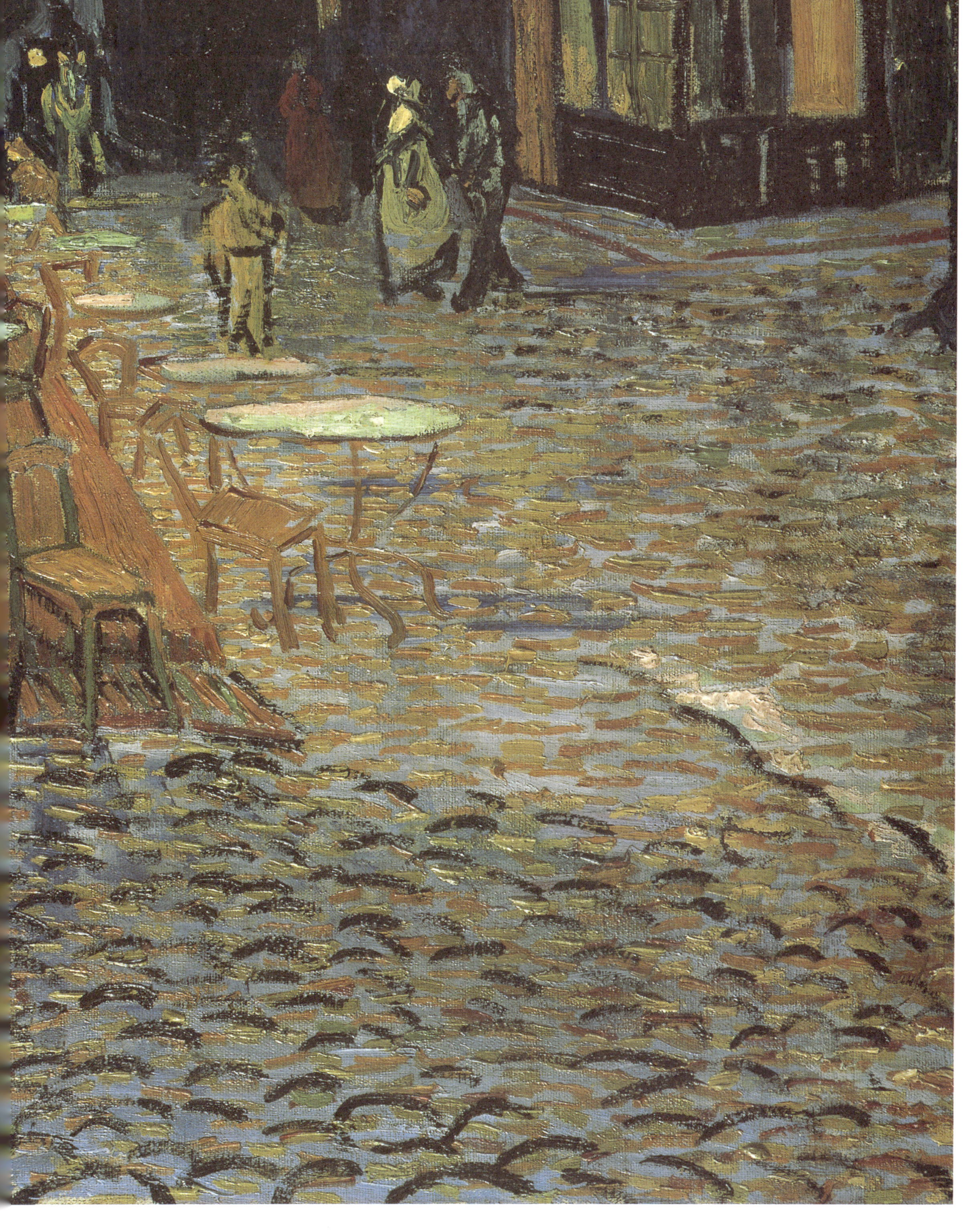

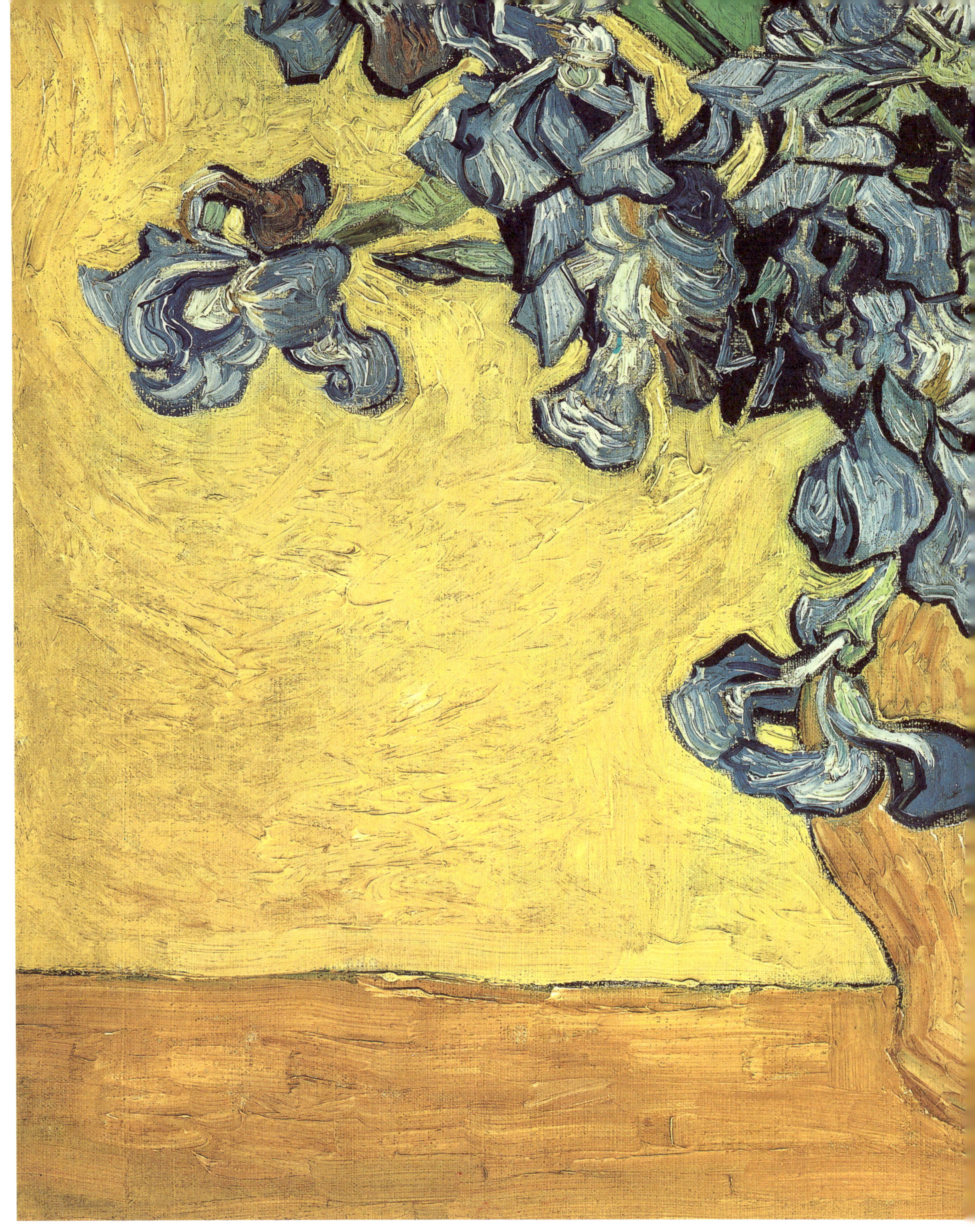

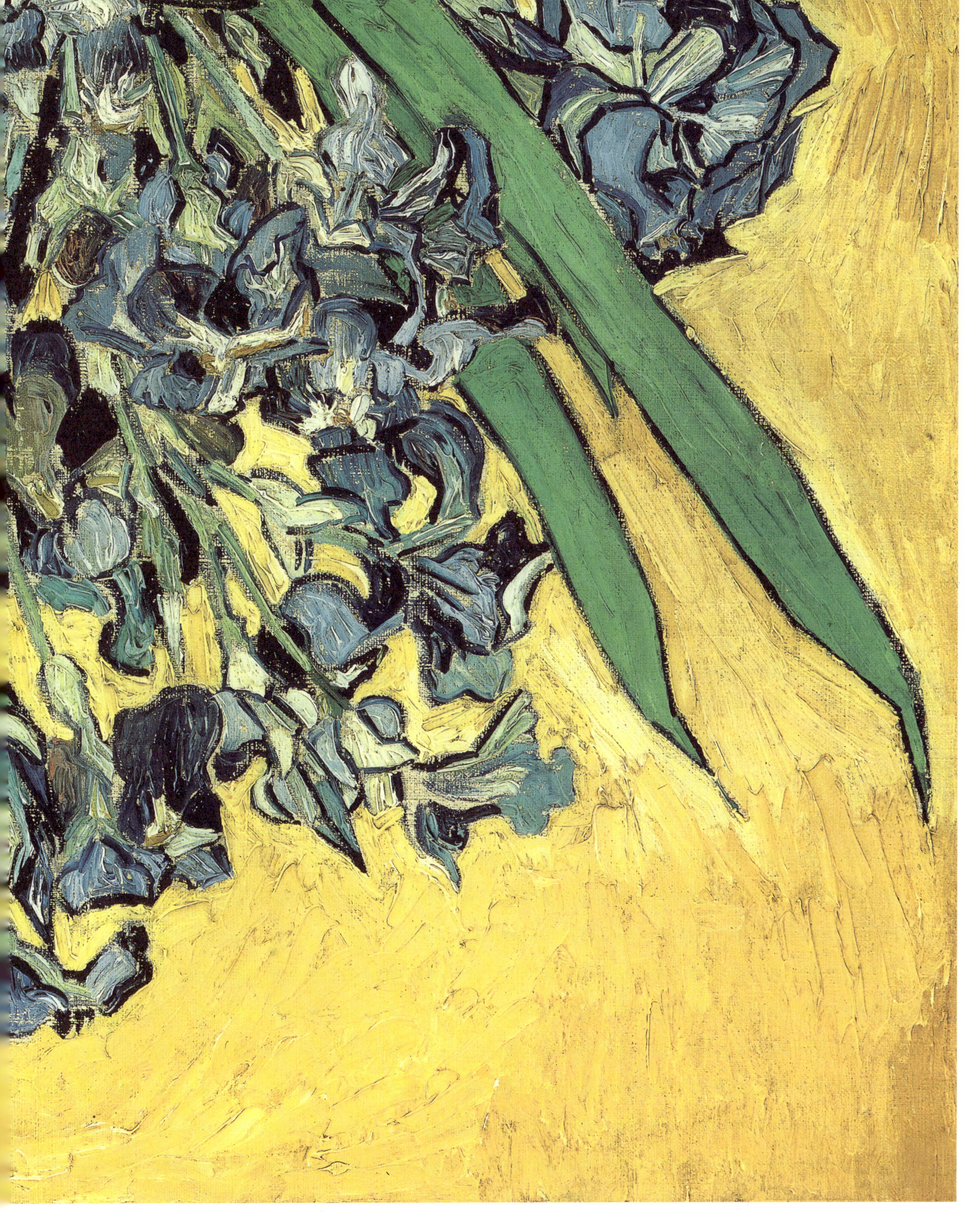

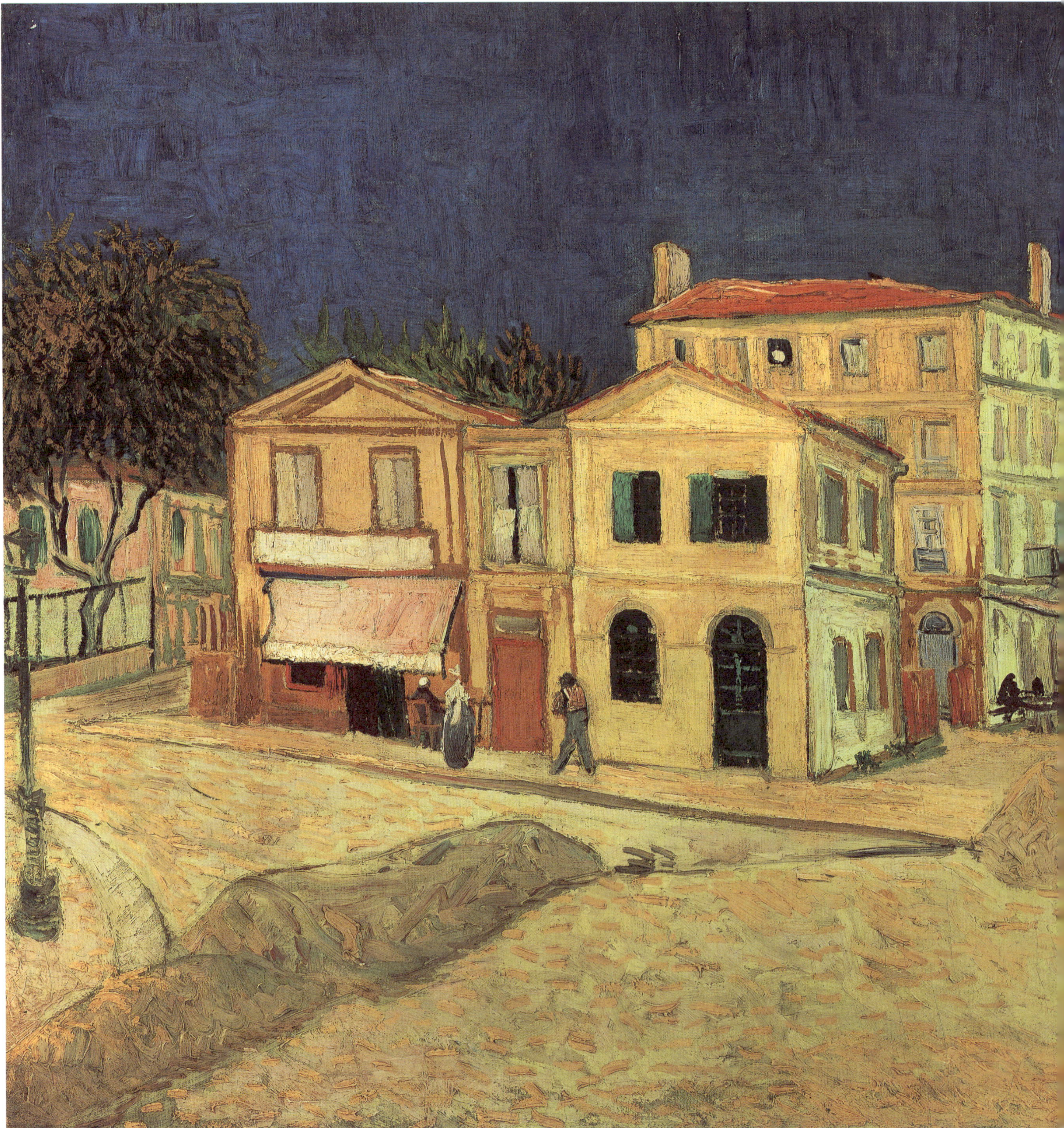

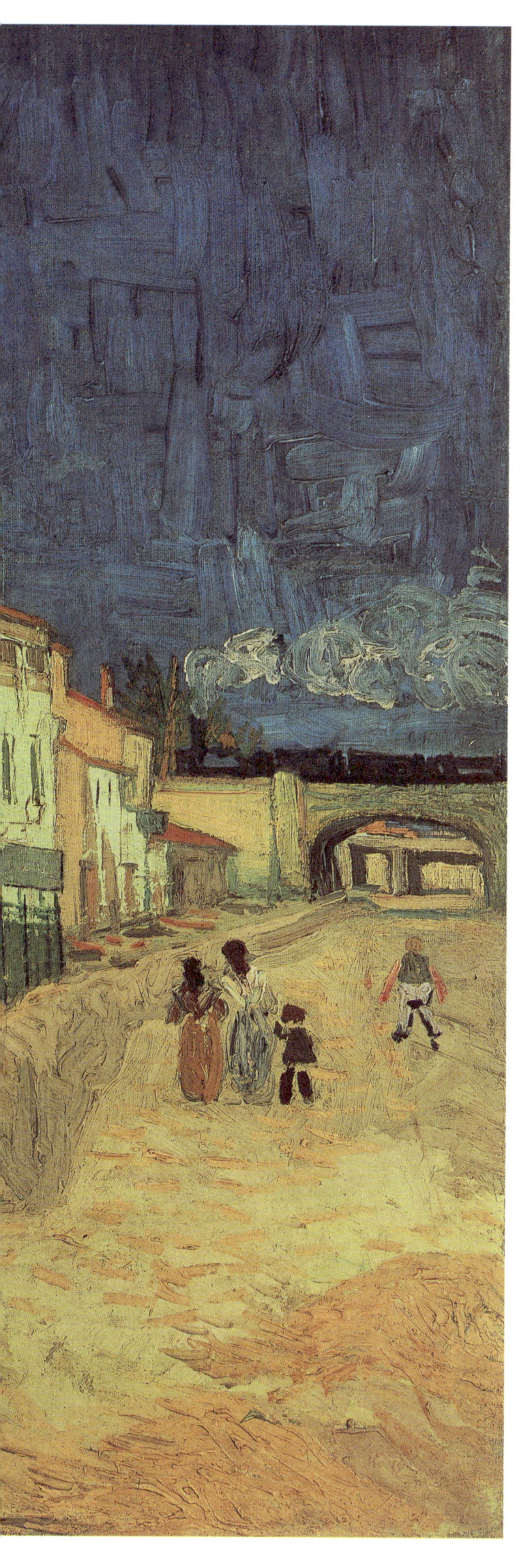

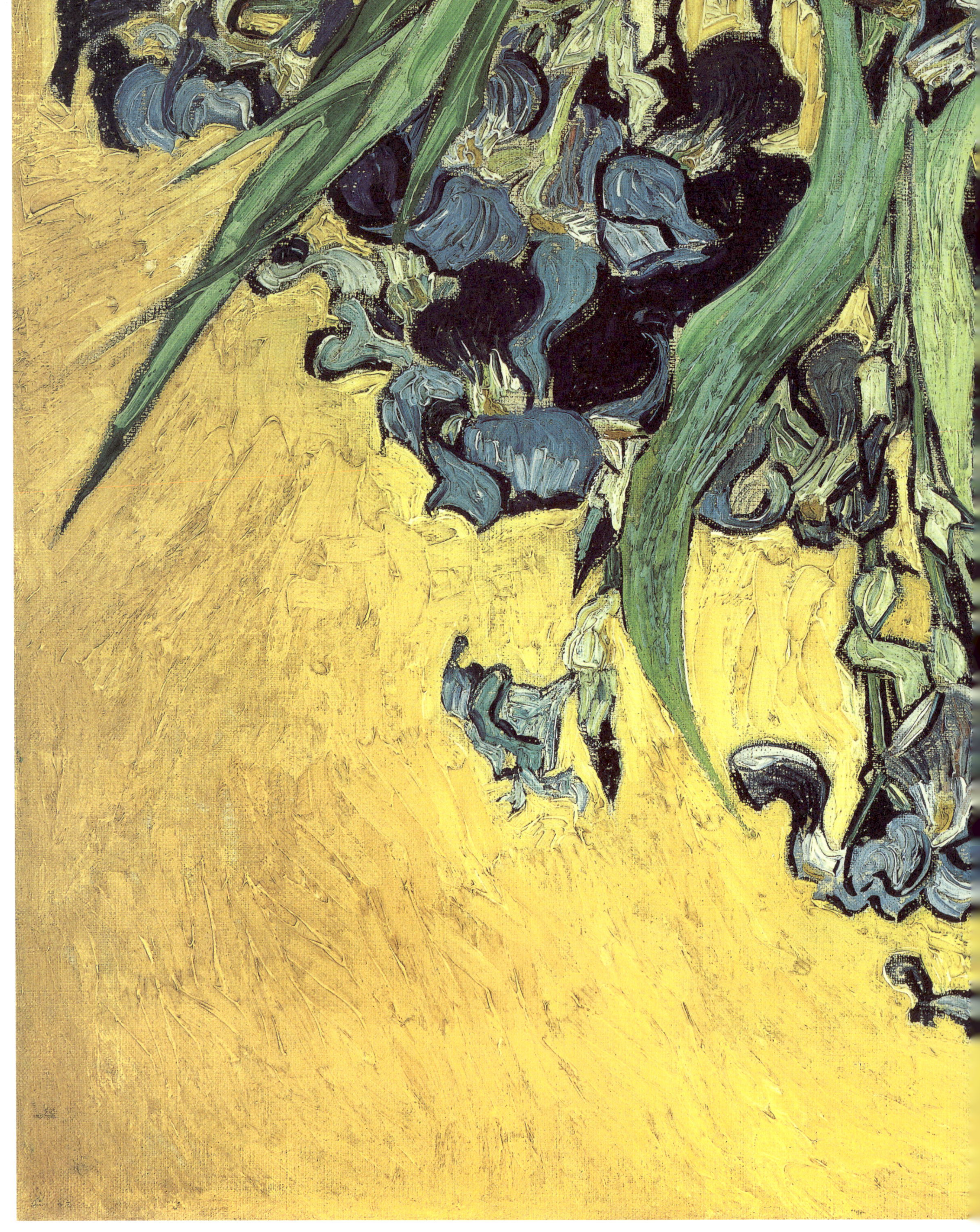

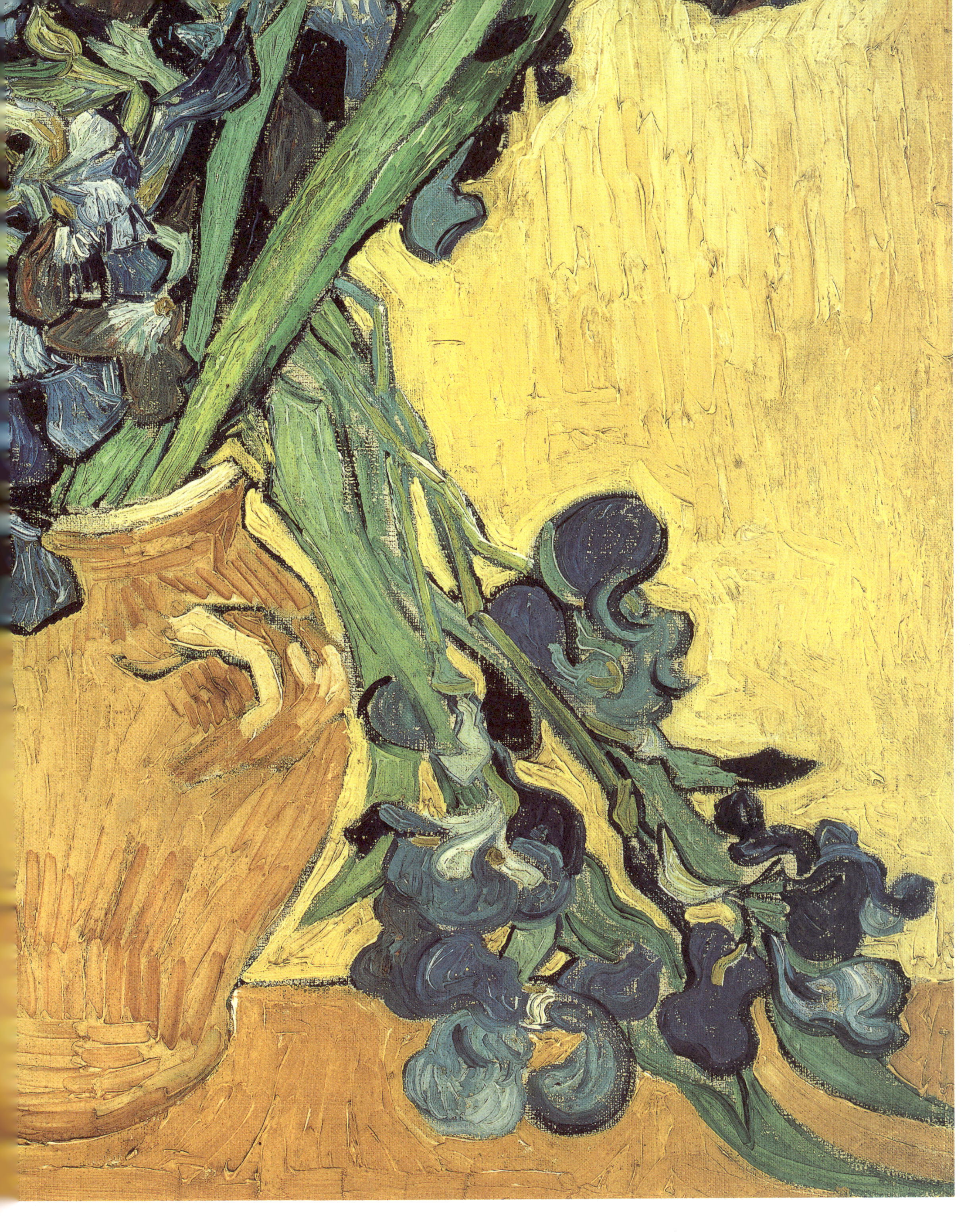

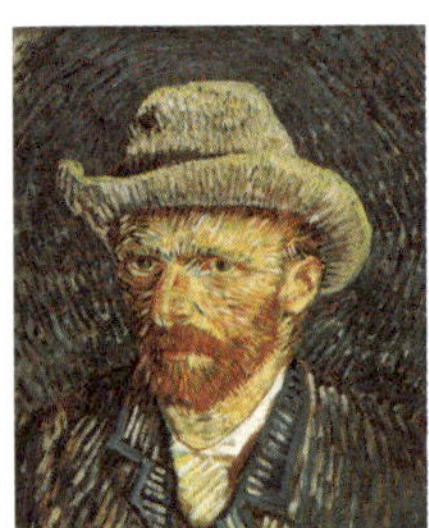

Self-Portrait with Felt Hat
1887-88, oil on canvas
44 × 37.5 cm
Vincent van Gogh Museum, Amsterdam—Vincent van Gogh Foundation

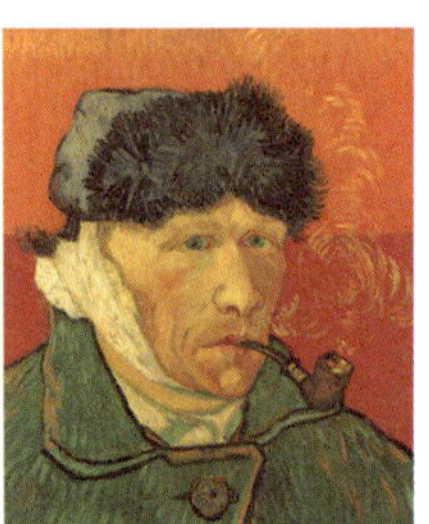

Self-Portrait with Bandaged Ear and Pipe
1889, oil on canvas
51 × 45 cm
Leigh B. Block collection, Chicago

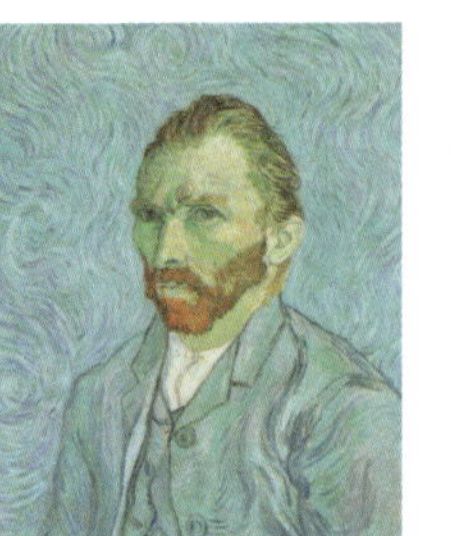

Portrait of the Artis
1889, oil on canvas
65 × 54.5 cm
Musée d'Orsay, Paris

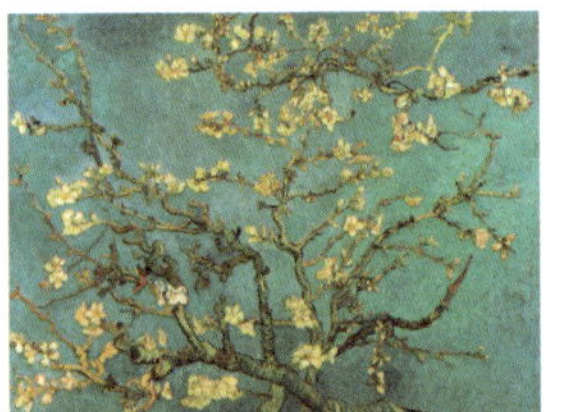

Almond Branches in Blossom
1890, oil on canvas
73.5 × 92 cm
Vincent van Gogh Museum, Amsterdam—Vincent van Gogh Foundation

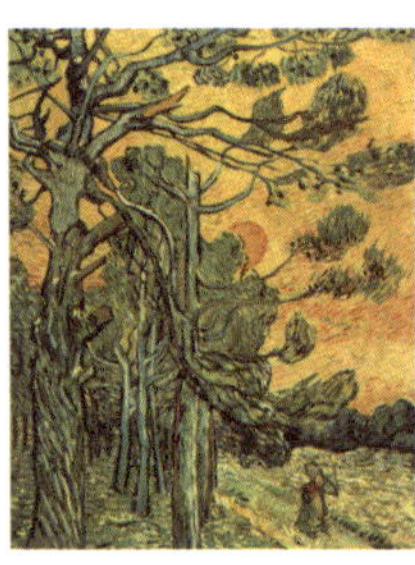

Pines at Sunset
1889, oil on canvas
92 × 73 cm
Kröller-Müller Museum, Otterlo

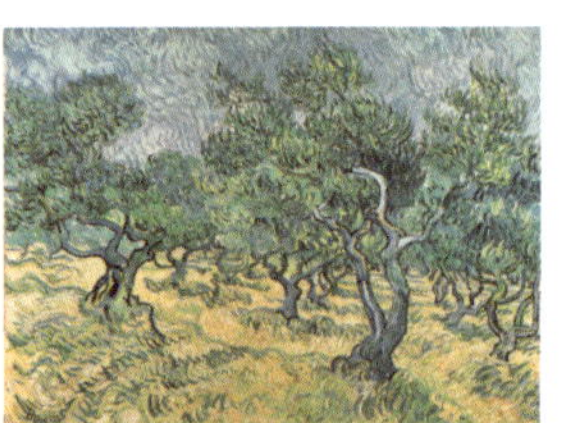

Olive Grove
1889, oil on canvas
72 × 92 cm
Kröller-Müller Museun
Otterlo

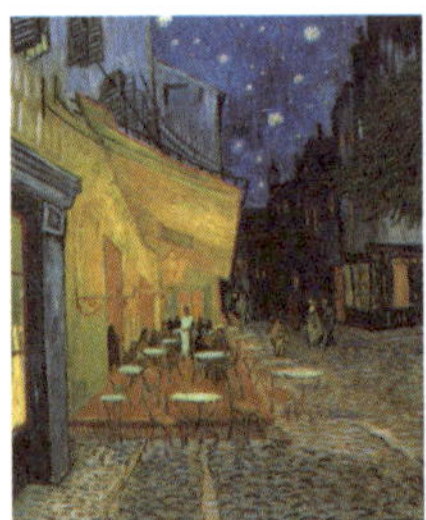

Terrace of the Café on the Place du Forum
1888, oil on canvas
81 × 65.5 cm
Kröller-Müller Museum, Otterlo

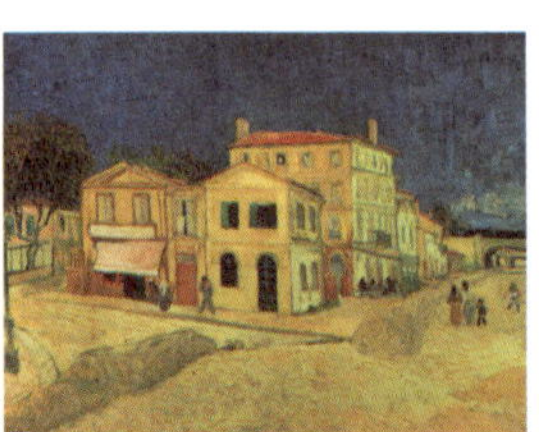

The Yellow House
1888, oil on canvas
72 × 91.5 cm
Vincent van Gogh Museum, Amsterdam—Vincent van Gogh Foundation

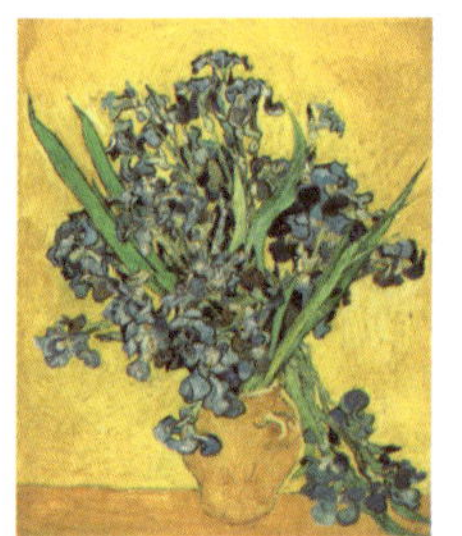

Irises
1890, oil on canvas
92 × 73.5 cm
Vincent van Gogh Museum, Amsterdam–Vincent van Gogh Foundation

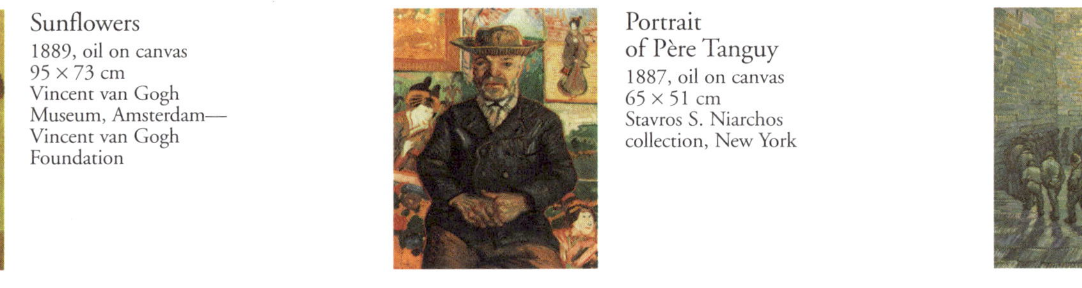

Sunflowers
1889, oil on canvas
95 × 73 cm
Vincent van Gogh
Museum, Amsterdam—
Vincent van Gogh
Foundation

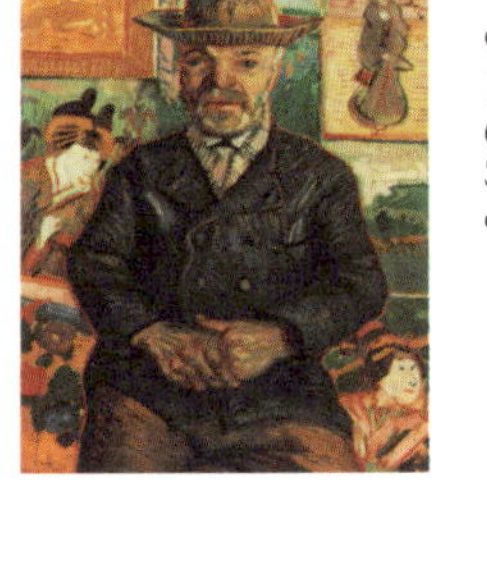

Portrait
of Père Tanguy
1887, oil on canvas
65 × 51 cm
Stavros S. Niarchos
collection, New York

Prisoners Exercising
1890, oil on canvas
80 × 64 cm
Pushkin Museum,
Moscow

The Harvest
1888, oil on canvas
72.5 × 92 cm
Vincent van Gogh
Museum, Amsterdam—
Vincent van Gogh
Foundation

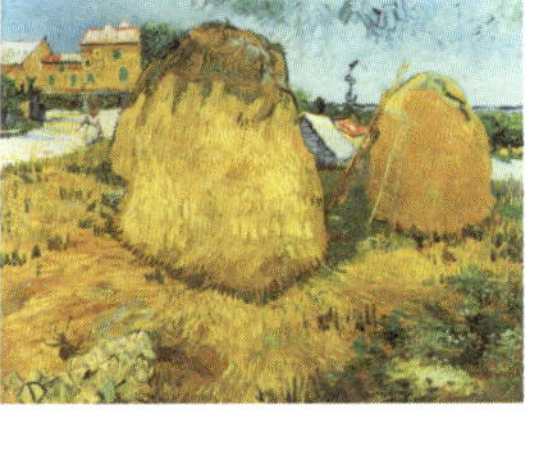

Haystacks
near a Farmhouse
1888, oil on canvas
73 × 92.5 cm
Kröller-Müller Museum,
Otterlo

The Night Café
1888, oil on canvas
70 × 89 cm
Yale University Art
Gallery, New Haven

La Berceuse
1889, oil on canvas
92 × 73 cm
Kröller-Müller Museum,
Otterlo

Portrait
of the Postman
Joseph Roulin
1889, oil on canvas
64 × 54.5 cm
Museum of Modern Art,
New York

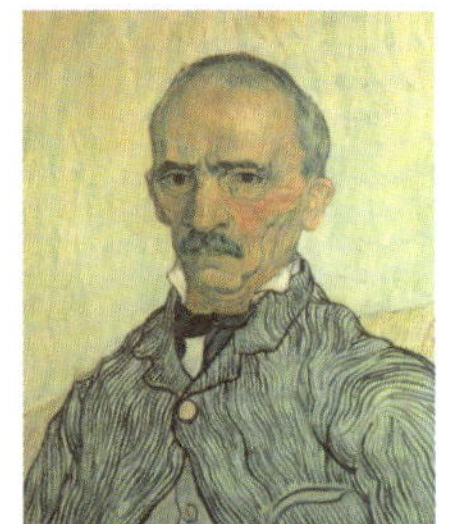
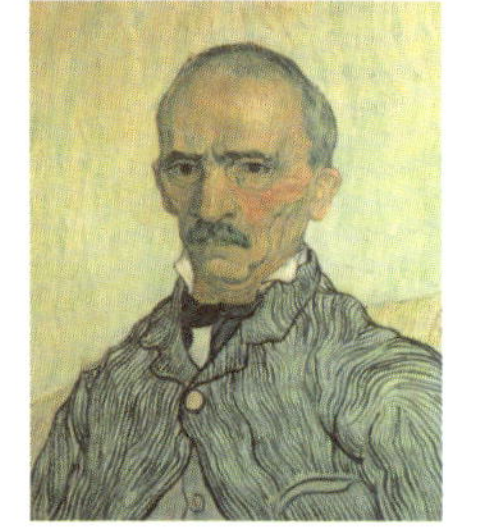
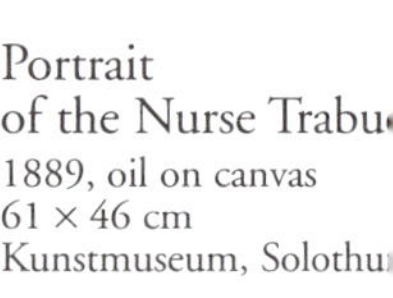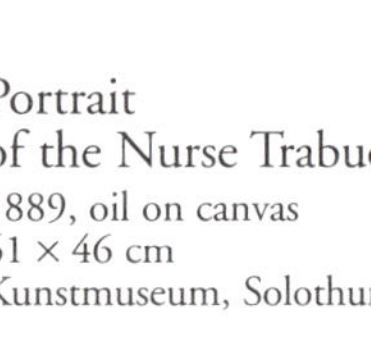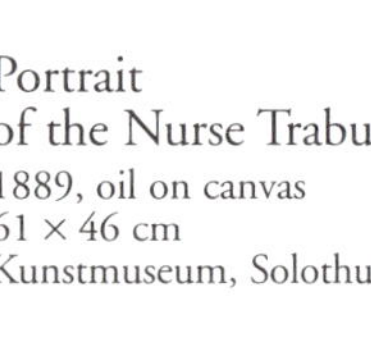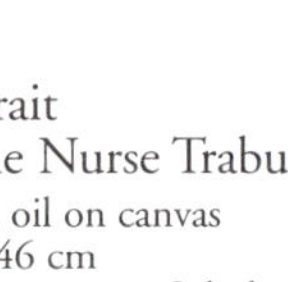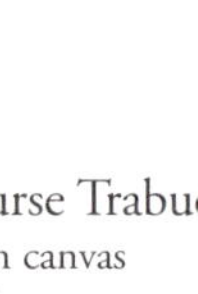

Portrait
of the Nurse Trabu
1889, oil on canvas
61 × 46 cm
Kunstmuseum, Solothu

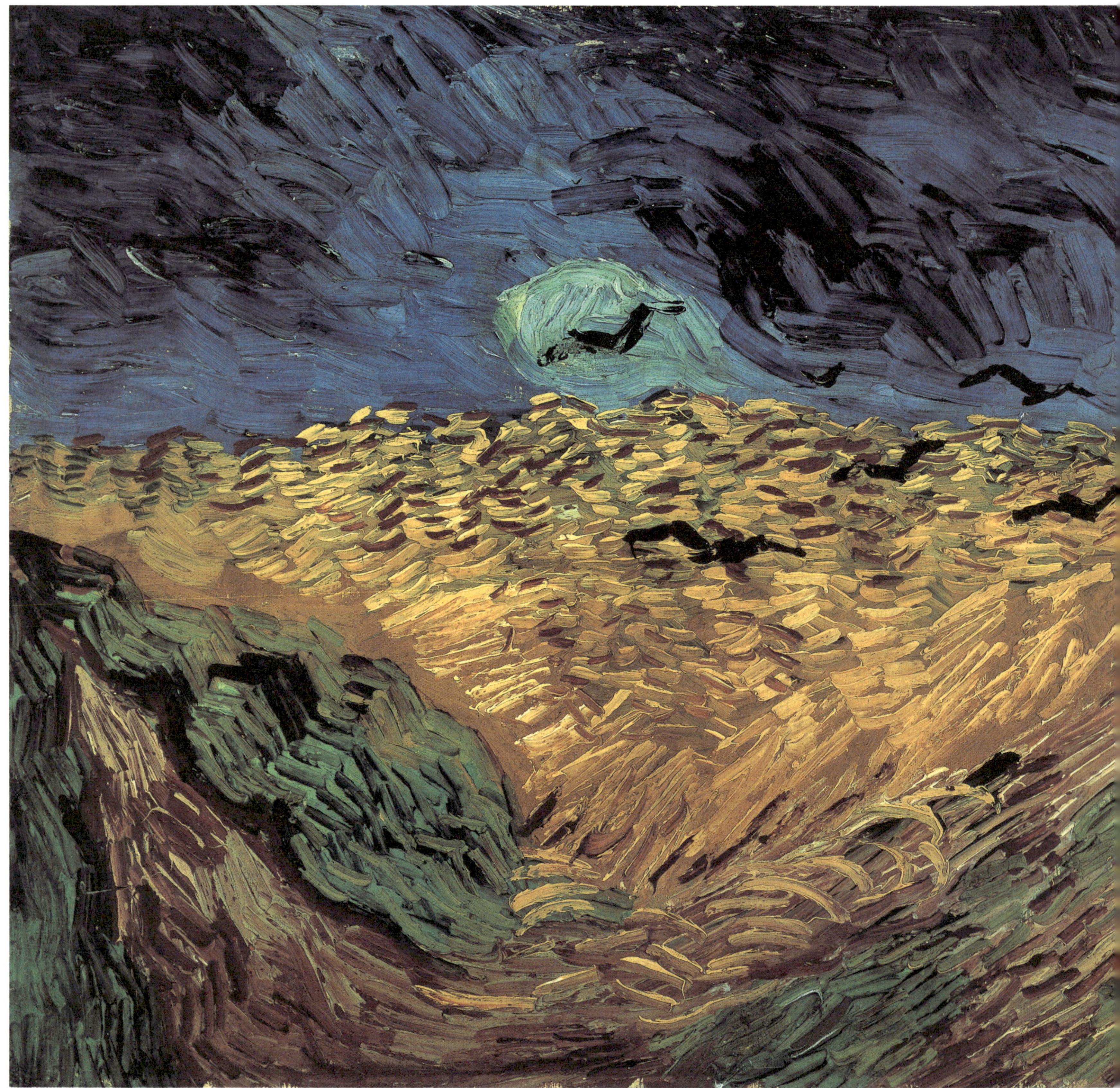

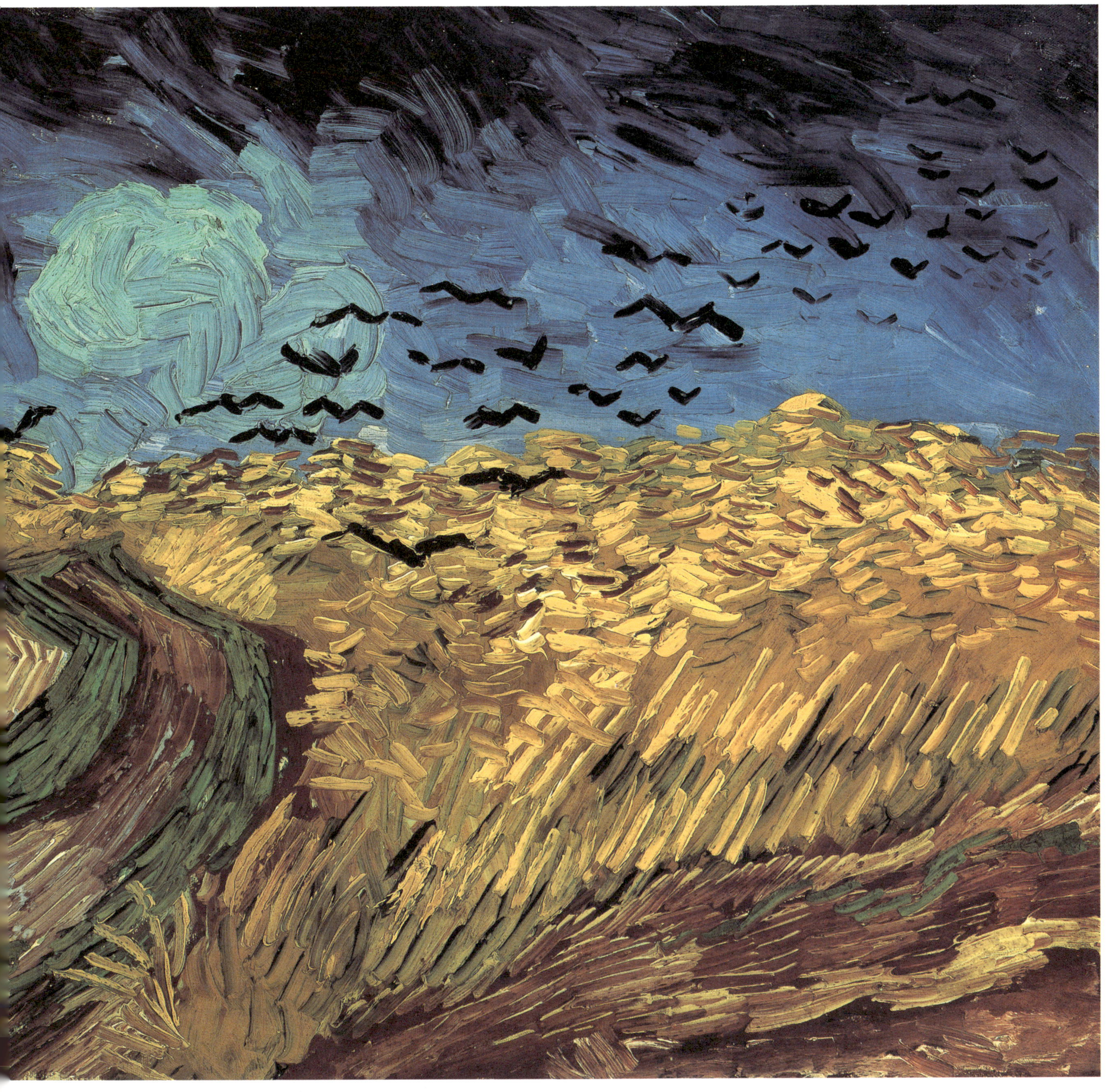

The Potato Eaters
1885, oil on canvas
81.5 × 114.5 cm
Vincent van Gogh
Museum, Amsterdam—
Vincent van Gogh
Foundation

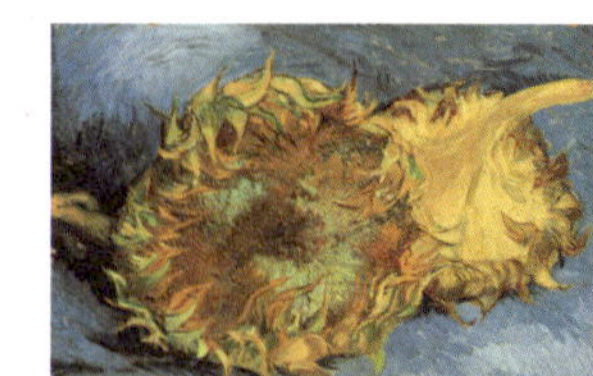
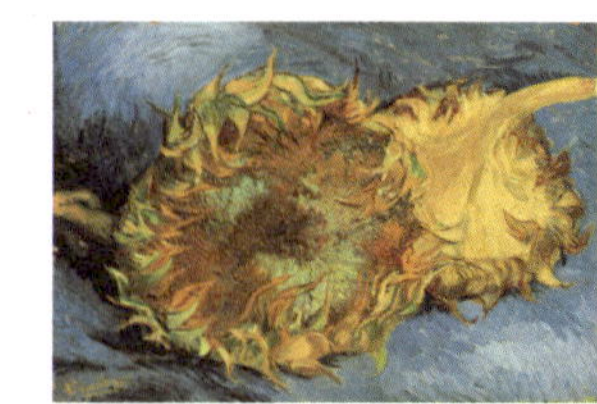
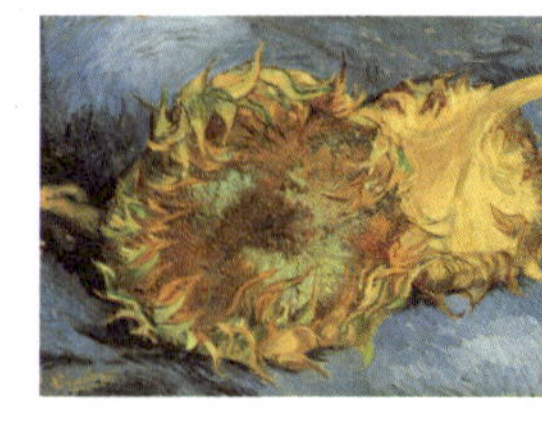

Sunflowers
1887, oil on canvas
43.2 × 61 cm
The Metropolitan
Museum of Art, New York

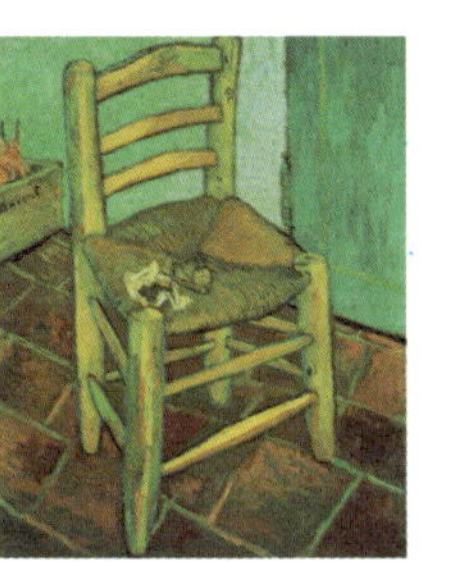

Van Gogh's Chair
1888, oil on canvas
93 × 73.5 cm
National Gallery, London

Portrait
of Dr. Paul Gachet
1890, oil on canvas
68 × 57 cm
Musée d'Orsay, Paris

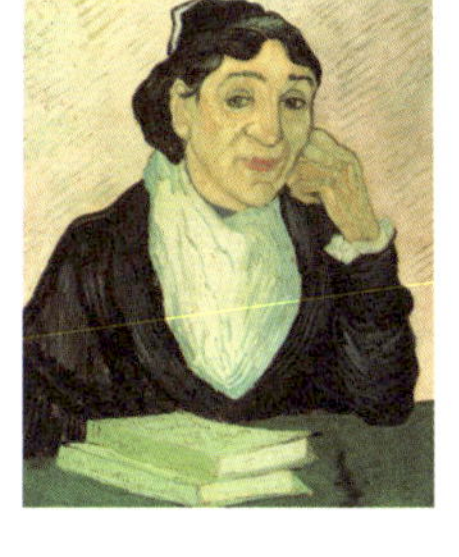

Portrait
of Madame Ginoux
(The Woman
of Arles)
1890, oil on canvas
65 × 49 cm
Kröller-Müller Museum,
Otterlo

Roulin the Postman
1888, oil on canvas
81.2 × 65.3 cm
Museum of Fine Arts,
Boston

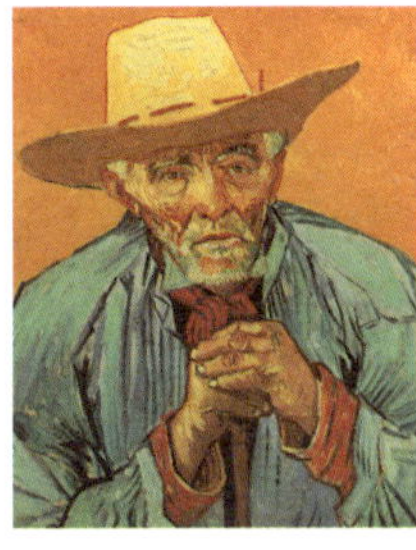

Portrait
of Patience Escalier
1888, oil on canvas
69 × 56 cm
Stavros S. Niarchos
collection, New York

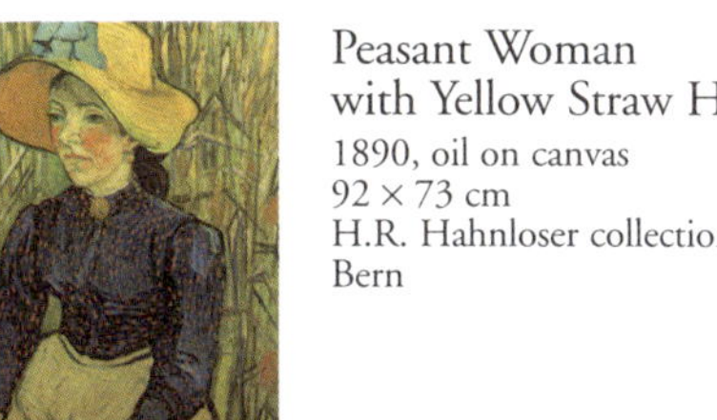

Peasant Woman
with Yellow Straw Hat
1890, oil on canvas
92 × 73 cm
H.R. Hahnloser collection,
Bern

Self-Portrait
with Shaved Head
1888, oil on canvas
62 × 52 cm
Fogg Art Museum,
Harvard University,
Cambridge

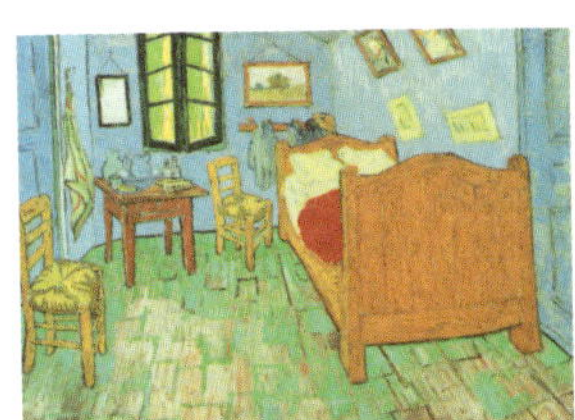

Bedroom
1889, oil on canvas
73 × 92 cm
Art Institute of Chicago, Chicago

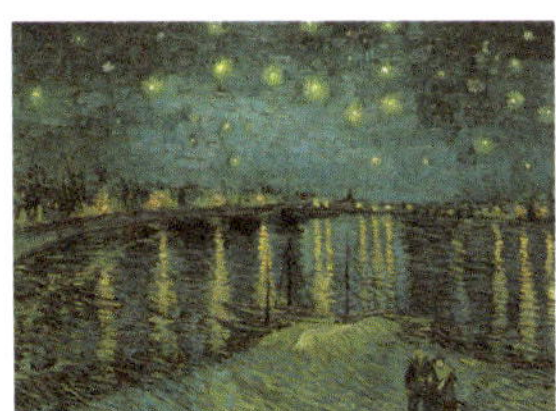

Starry Night above the Rhône
1888, oil on canvas
72.5 × 92 cm
Musée d'Orsay, Paris

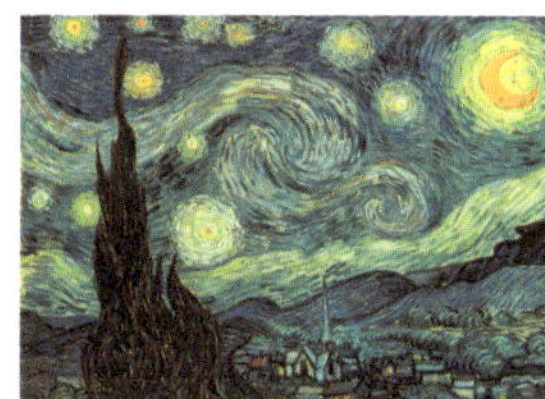

Starry Night
1889, oil on canvas
73 × 92 cm
Museum of Modern Art, New York

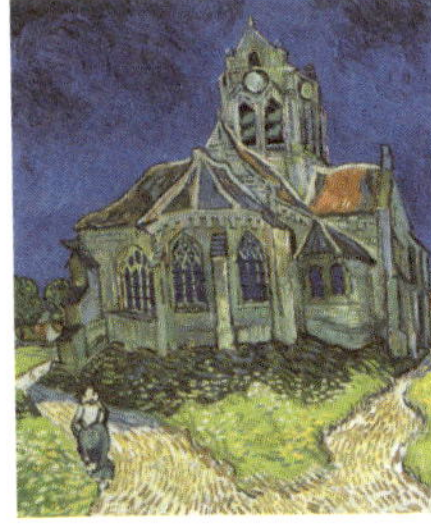

Church at Auvers-sur-Oise
1890, oil on canvas
94 × 74.5 cm
Musée d'Orsay, Paris

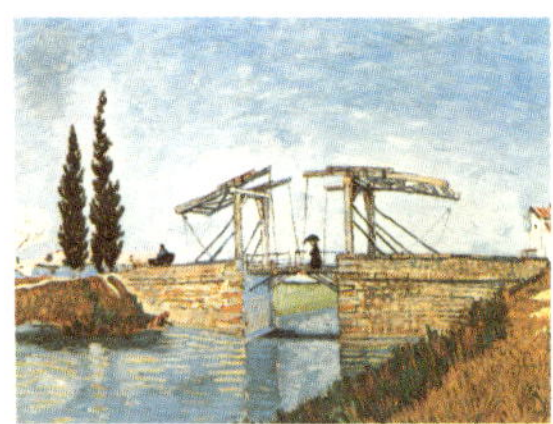

The Bridge at Langlois
1888, oil on canvas
51 × 67 cm
Wallraf-Richartz Museum, Cologne

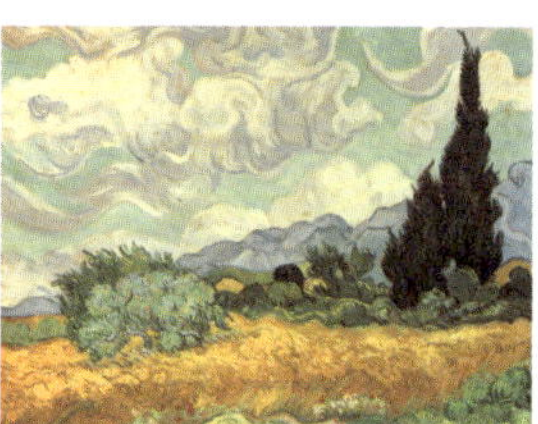

Wheatfield with Cypresses
1889, oil on canvas
72.5 × 91.5 cm
National Gallery, London

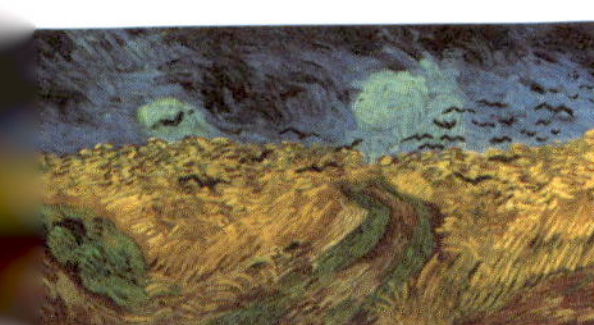

Wheatfield with Crows
1890, oil on canvas
50.5 × 103 cm
Vincent van Gogh Museum, Amsterdam—Vincent van Gogh Foundation

Vincent Van Gogh

edited by
Francesca Castria Marchetti

Photographic credits

Archivio Electa, Milan
Agence photographique de la Reunion
des Musées Nationaux, Paris

We would also like to thank the galleries and private individuals who have supplied photographic material.

First published in the United States by
Rizzoli International Publications, Inc.
300 Park Avenue South
New York, NY 10010

ISBN 0-8478-2311-3
LC 00-102590

Printed in Italy

Octavius
Registered trademark, model and concept
Gallimard-Zanardi